*The Secret Life of a Fool* reminds us of the rebellion created when we buy into the world's definition of "kick 'em up party fun." It grooms a life of exponential selfishness, arrogance, and self-indulgence. I know because I've been there. *The Secret Life of a Fool* is the sometimes pitiful and sometimes shocking story of Andrew Palau, son of my good friend Luis Palau. But Andrew didn't write this story for shock value. He has written it because of his overwhelming desire for everyone to know of God's universal offer of love, forgiveness, freedom, blessing, hope, and purpose. This is a remarkable story of a radically changed life.

NORM MILLER
Chairman, Interstate Batteries


I have known the Palau family for over twenty years. I saw Luis's pain — that of a father watching his son descend further and further from sight. But Andrew Palau's story is one of good news, for it shows both the diligent work of a loving earthly father (and mother), as well as that of our heavenly Father, refusing to give up the search for his son. This is a remarkable rescue story that you won't be able to put down, because we've either experienced it or are in the middle of it in our own ways—a loving God offering freedom from guilt and a hope for a future. I'm not surprised Andrew has finally penned his story, for every time I have heard it told, it is through the teary eyes of a broken man who only desires that others will understand the grace and mercy offered by our loving God.

JOHN DALTON
Former Secretary of the Navy


Here is a story in which we can each see our own story and be encouraged. There is hope. We are not alone in the universe. God is waiting to welcome us. Don't wait a moment longer.

OS GUINNESS
Founder of Trinity Forum and author of *Long Journey Home*

Andrew Palau's story is a gripping reminder of what happens when we live for ourselves. It's the story of a young man descending into a deep pit of hopelessness and despair, only to be rescued under the most ironic of circumstances. Andrew's story shows how a merciful, loving God offers to each of us forgiveness, peace, and a future. It is a powerful, engaging story of hope that will encourage every reader.

MIKE HUCKABEE
Former governor of Arkansas, *New York Times* best-selling author, radio and TV commentator

The safest way to navigate a minefield is to follow the guy who has already walked through it and survived. If your minefield is drugs, alcohol, or doing everything you can to run away from God, then Andrew Palau is your guide. Trust him; he knows the way out.

DAVE RAMSEY
*New York Times* best-selling author and nationally syndicated radio host

This book has both *guts* and *grace*. Andrew Palau guides us through his story with such a raw honesty—and yet all the dark moments and detours along the way are ultimately overshadowed by one thing: the beautiful grace of God. It's a compelling read, and a wonderful reminder that there is no heart so distant that it cannot be reached by the majestic mercy of Jesus.

MATT REDMAN
Songwriter and worship leader

This is not just another bad-boy-finds-salvation-in-Jesus story. Rather, it is an honest account of God's patience through the bad years. I'm happy to have this book in my personal library and can easily recommend it to others.

AL EGG
Beyond Victory Ministries, Portland Trailblazers team chaplain

Andrew Palau tells an extraordinary story. The son of one of the world's most renowned evangelists, he drifted into a life of drugs and alcohol, only to find forgiveness and new life in Jesus Christ at one of his father's missions. This is a story of hope.

REV. NICKY GUMBEL
Alpha chaplain, Vicar of Holy Trinity—Brompton, and author


Jesus once looked into the soul of a woman guilty of more than her share of sins. He saw something nobody around her could see—the reality that her years of sin made her more ready and grateful for God's forgiveness than most. Andrew's story is a lot like that. Through a lens of uncompromising honesty, he lets us look into a life enslaved to sin. The effect is heart-wrenching, but it reminds us that God's forgiveness is limitless, and that those who've been forgiven much, love much . . . and are often those who proclaim Him most powerfully. Whether you're the praying parent of a prodigal, a believer who hasn't totally surrendered to God's will, or a sinner seeking to be set free, Andrew's "fool's life" is sure to encourage and enable you to take the next necessary step with God.

PASTOR BOB COY
Calvary Chapel of Fort Lauderdale, Florida

# THE SECRET LIFE OF A FOOL

ONE MAN'S RAW JOURNEY FROM SHAME TO GRACE

## BY ANDREW PALAU

**WORTHY**
PUBLISHING

Published by Worthy Publishing, a division of Worthy Media, Inc., 134 Franklin Road, Suite 200, Brentwood, Tennessee 37027.

HELPING PEOPLE EXPERIENCE THE HEART OF GOD

eBook available at www.worthypublishing.com

Audio distributed through Oasis Audio; visit www.oasisaudio.com

Library of Congress Control Number: 2012932499

Published in association with Yates & Yates, LLP; www.yates2.com

For foreign and subsidiary rights, contact Riggins International Rights Services, Inc.; www.rigginsrights.com

ISBN: 978-1-936034-76-5 (trade paper)

Cover Design: Faceout Studio / Jeff Miller
Cover Image: Tyler Gould
Interior Design and Typesetting: Juicebox Designs / Kristi Smith

Printed in the United States of America

12 13 14 15 16 17 18 RRD  9 8 7 6 5 4 3 2

This book is dedicated to my mother, Patricia Palau.
Thanks, Mom! I love you.

*But by the grace of God, I am what I am,*
*and His grace to me was not without effect.*

*1 Corinthians 15:10*

# CONTENTS

# FOREWORD

ANDREW PALAU AND I are complete opposites; we go about most everything differently. Andrew dives in with pure passion, while I am a methodical perfectionist. Andrew plans life, while I let life plan me. Andrew truly rebelled early in life, while I truly wanted to please authority. He's a West Coast kid —flannel shirts and fly fishing—while I'm all East Coast, baby. Andrew loves to serve his friends, while I love to be served. He is impatient, while I can be patient with his impatience. Andrew is quick-witted, while I'm still processing. He loves college football, and I'm an NFL'er. Andrew loves the great outdoors; I love a fast break on the hardwood floor.

We came together by marriage, with both of us marrying into the stratosphere, a.k.a. waaay above our heads. Two beautiful, God-loving Jamaican sisters. They are storybook, to be sure—from a family that has taught me so much about really walking with God in all that it is and all that it is not. But that's another story for another time.

Every Christmas at our in-laws' house in the hills of Kingston, Jamaica, Andrew and I would sit poolside, swapping stories and pondering life. I quickly learned that my "crazy" stories of being brought up in metropolitan DC and touring during my dc Talk days paled in comparison to Andrew's upbringing in the great Northwest in the home of an evangelist. Honestly, I stopped telling and started listening, captivated by his amazingly irresponsible acts of recreation. Even his fairly innocent elementary school stories showed a creative deviance that demanded my respect. And as the stories kept pouring out of his mouth, I found myself somewhere between rolling on the floor in laughter and sitting in silence as Andrew would be suddenly overwhelmed with remorse. What struck me in those moments was that the same passion that drove those delinquent acts was now being turned into compassion for the pain he had caused and the people he had mistreated.

That's when I began to really know Andrew and, more importantly, learn his story. A story that I've always felt he should share. When I encouraged him, he was reluctant, of course. Who wouldn't be? Most of us can't imagine the foolish acts of our youth being in black and white for all to see . . . Who wants to sit through a seven-year-old Michael Jordan "gettin' it wrong" for hours on the court down the street from his house? We want to watch him in full bloom, winning championships and flying.

It's kind of how I feel about dc Talk's "I love rap music" video: some embarrassments simply aren't meant for public consumption.

Nobody is comfortable with you listening to their immature sounds—a garage band is a garage band for a reason. Most of us burn our demo tapes when we sign a deal. Once we are properly made up and auto-tuned, we are presented to the public in a marketable fashion. But when someone is generous enough to allow you to look into the unedited raw footage of their life, it somehow offers us hope.

I love the way Eugene Peterson put it in his book, *Christ Plays in Ten Thousand Places*: "Our stories are verbal acts of hospitality." Andrew, as a beautiful act of service, has invited us into his story. You may laugh; you may cringe; but I hope that, like myself, you are amazed by the patient, painstaking way in which God pursues us through other people.

tobyMac
January 2012

# ONE
# FOUR SECONDS TO LIFE

Open your eyes, look within.
Are you satisfied with the life you're living?

—Bob Marley


SOMETHING WAS WRONG. We were going too fast. Or it was raining too hard—the pilots couldn't see. What was going on?

I knew that when there's bad weather, pilots work the reverse thrusters extra hard, but something seemed off. I just couldn't tell what. My eyes darted around the cabin from the other passengers to my family sitting in the seats on either side of me. Some passengers looked tense, some looked nonchalant, and some were even applauding the odd landing.

*Are you kidding? You're gonna clap for that landing?*

Confusion and doubt fired through my mind. I knew this runway. I knew there was only a chain-link fence between the end of the pavement and the beginning of the Caribbean Sea.

Then it happened.

The impact was immense. My face slammed into the seat in front of me, gashing my forehead right above my nose. There was blood and pain and darkness.

Pitch black for three or four seconds, and then the lights flickered on. In the midst of the confusion, I felt as though I'd fallen asleep in a movie theater and awoken during a difficult scene. I couldn't decipher fact from fiction. One moment everything was clean and tidy and in its place. Then, in an instant, everything changed. It was just wires, panels, and luggage strewn everywhere.

My first thought was, *I'm alive.* The next thought was the sickening horror of it: *I'm alive, but is anyone else alive—my boys, my daughter, my wife?* In that moment you don't want to know the answer. Everything was quiet. My heart sank, and then leapt in my chest as movement came from under the pile of debris to my left. My boys were okay. I turned to find the girls alive as well. Next thought: *Get out of here!*

I could see some people beginning to move around. Most were still huddled in their seats. The dim emergency lighting flickered on, casting an eerie glow while rain blew into the exposed cabin. The massive 737 lay broken, the rain pounding on the three pieces.

The seconds it took to figure out what happened seemed like an eternity. But then the slow motion of time caught up with the reality of the situation. People began to panic.

"It's going to be okay!" I shouted. "Take it easy. Leave everything. Let's just get out of here. Everyone, stay calm!"

I tried to calm the situation but found little success against the mounting surge among the passengers that had turned to full panic. People began to realize what had happened. I helped my two boys, Christopher and Jonathan, out from the wires and panels on top of them.

Sadie, my two-year-old daughter, was in her car seat. We never travel with a car seat. For all the times coming to Jamaica with the boys, we never brought it along. The one time my wife, Wendy, convinced me to bring it, this happens. And to think how frustrated and obstinate I had been about bringing it.

I always thought, *I have them; I can hold them. They'll be okay.* But in that instant I realized that nothing is safe and with all my strength I could never protect them from forces like a plane crash.

I think of what could have been if we had left the car seat behind. Wendy or I would have been holding Sadie. I think of my face—swollen and bleeding. If I had been holding her . . . my mind flashes through this scenario and I shudder. I'm thanking God. I'm grabbing Sadie. I'm gathering my family.

Rob, the soldier who sat behind me, is helping us out onto the wing. This is now. This is my reality.

But all the panic in the cabin didn't last long. Rob took control.

"Okay. Take it easy, everyone. No pushing. Calm down and move toward the exits." He delivered these lines as though he had experienced it all before. Rob was a hero in the moment, a serviceman coming home to his family for Christmas. Now, serving us—the panicked and afraid.

I gathered my family on the wing and we stood looking out into the night. How far down was it? Was it ten feet? Twenty feet? I couldn't see. It was dark and rainy, but there I stood on an airplane wing with my family about to jump. I *can't believe I'm going to jump off the wing of this plane.*

But I've always been ready to survive. When my brothers and I were younger we had our little metal lunchbox that we turned into our survival kit. We were survivors. Right? I was a long way from that survival kit. Survival wasn't such a cool and innocent thing now. It was simple necessity.

Before my eyes adjusted to the depth of field, Jonathan noticed that the wing was only one foot off the ground. "What are we waiting for?" he asked.

I could see the landing gear and the jet engine on the right side had completely torn away. The plane lay on its belly and leaned to the right. We just had to step off the wing onto the jagged honeycomb rocks and sand.

Brilliant.

The sand? Where were we?

I was laughing at my thoughts, crying through the rain.

*Thank You, God. Thank You, God. Thank You, God.*

We were among the first to step foot on land—confusion behind us but uncertainty before us. I just wanted to huddle and hold my family. My mind kept racing as the rain soaked us.

A memory from my childhood popped into my racing thoughts. It was a bizarre memory to be emerging at this moment: a memory of a vision I had at my grandma's house when I was a boy. My cousins came over to play with my brothers and me. Everyone ran inside to get a drink. As I lingered behind and found myself alone in the large yard, my eye caught something in the sky. I looked up and saw something incredible and golden up above Portland's West Hills. I could not tell if it was real or just my imagination playing games with me. It was also Easter weekend, which made everything seem even stranger . . . or maybe stronger?

There was this breaking cloud and inside of the cloud I saw a golden city— fantasy-like in its simplicity. I was struck by how tangible the vision was. And so I waited for what seemed like an hour for one of my brothers or cousins to come back out and see this shimmering city with me. But no one came.

I didn't want to take my eyes off it, but I finally ran into the house to get someone—anyone—to confirm it was real. But when I came back out the city had vanished. I've often thought about that childhood vision. It was a simple seed that God gave me as if to say, "This is what is real. I am real. Will you believe Me?"

In that harrowing moment after the crash, the glimmering city surfaced again. It invaded my consciousness, my life seeming to move in slow motion while my thoughts continued to run wild.

I had to get my bearings, but I had to get my family away

from the wreckage—the smell of jet fuel was overpowering. Jonathan was only wearing socks. Would he injure his feet? Sadie was shivering in my arms—cold and wet. Was she going into shock? Was she cut or bleeding? With my sons in front of me, Wendy behind me, I carried Sadie and began moving us away from the plane.

*Where are we?* I thought. We were walking among the rocks and shrubs and sand. *We must be on the beach.* I kept walking, guiding my family further away from the wreckage. Sadie clung to me—her head buried in my neck.

Just as we began to gain confidence and picked up the pace of our escape, we discovered that we were mere feet from the ocean. The shoreline was right in front of us. The waves crashed violently at our feet. My family was safe with just minor scrapes and bruises. But we had to get farther away from the plane. Not only could I smell the jet fuel, I could see it pouring from the plane. More scared thoughts.

*Many survive the crash but die in the fire.*

We headed away from the sea toward what I thought looked like a gully. We slowed as we approached it. It looked deep and I could see water flowing in it. Then I saw lights in the distance.

*Oh, it's Palisadoes Road,* I thought.

We were about fifteen feet above the road. As we made our way down toward the road, lights in the distance moved closer. It was a city bus. Wendy waved her arms and flagged it down. The driver looked surprised to see a plane so close to the road. She looked at me, smiling in an attempt to mask her confusion. Her eyes said, *Am I in some strange movie? What I'm seeing doesn't make sense.* The gravity of the situation finally registered on her face. The fact that my family was bloodied and bruised and wet and that more people were emerging from the dark shore also gave her a clue.

Everyone clambered onto the bus. When I made sure my family was safely aboard, I felt as if I could breathe again—as if I had been holding my breath for the past ten minutes. The bus was full but far from calm. Many shouted for the driver to get them out of there. We left as emergency vehicles came and gathered up those remaining.

My family sat dazed and thankful to be alive and together. As the bus drove off, I sang a familiar song we often sang together. "Jesus, Name above all names, beautiful Savior, glorious Lord. Emmanuel, God is with us . . ."[1]

And He was.

## TWO
# WATCHING IT BURN

If I set down every action in my life and every thought that has crossed my mind, the world would consider me a monster of depravity.

—Somerset Maugham

I USUALLY READ stories like the one about our plane crash the way you do. I read about the US Airways flight 1549 that ended up in the Hudson River and remember thinking, *What a miracle. What a great pilot! What must those people have thought during the process? What must they have learned? To have come so close to death and yet walk away unscathed—how sweet life must taste to them now.*

But then, like you, I turn the page of the newspaper before reading the details and continue with breakfast. "Pass the marmalade, please. Yes, I'd love some more coffee."

But that evening, on a sliver of beach in Jamaica, I was living it and there was no skipping the details. There I stood, a few feet from the Caribbean Sea holding my two-year-old daughter in my arms with my boys and wife at my side. The only thought at that point is: *I'm grateful for our lives.* In a situation like that your mind races to what could have happened: *We could have slammed into an embankment! Or what if we skidded into the sea?* Then, to what *did* happen. Then to your family again—how much you love them. It's all quite huge in your brain, and it remains huge for months.

When that plane broke apart, life crystallized for me. More than ever, I *knew* that God holds this world, and everything that happens, in His hand—good and bad. More than ever, I understood the most important things in life carry a deep significance; they transcend the everyday and change you—things like love, things you put your faith in, family, and your life's calling. More than ever, I could see the fragility of life; how quickly we can and do pass like a vapor.

But what are we doing within that vapor? Which moments of the in-between sections—the living sections—define us and point us toward real life for *now* and for *eternity?* These questions stuck in my brain.

My family's experience on the plane was serious and shocking, but thankfully no one died. Maybe most of all, it was jarring. It forced us—and me the most—to consider the hard and true thoughts about life. Was I living a life that, if snuffed out in a plane crash, would leave a sweet aroma representative of what matters most?

At that time, there wasn't long to reflect because, by morning, I had numerous news organizations and television and radio stations calling my father-in-law's cell phone for the story. But since then, I've had plenty of time to think about it. In fact, my entire life has been stamped with colorful events: from that plane crash near the Caribbean Sea to burning cars at frat parties in college to wandering in Europe with a buddy to falling on my knees in the Jamaican Blue Mountains calling out to God. It's lined with innocence, guilt, and all that falls in between. It's a breath away from being completely tragic and a gulp of pride away from being completely beautiful. Ironically, the dark rain that night on the beach after the crash helped me see all this more clearly. It has helped me see my story in light of eternity.

One minute you're daydreaming about what beach you're going to be sunning yourself on and the next minute you're on that beach in the middle of a midnight rainstorm staring into the darkness trying to get away from a crumpled airplane.

Nothing prepares you for life better than brushing against death. And life exists in fleeting moments—moments that carve us into the men and women we are and will be. I remember thinking how time froze in the confusion of the landing and crashing. As though God held His breath and reached out His hand, especially for those seconds as the airplane careened over the road and crashed on the shoreline. One-one-thousand—you sense something wrong. Two-one-thousand—sudden impact, blackness, screams. Three-one-thousand—awful thoughts about losing your family, losing your life, losing it all. Four-one-thousand—*we're here, we're all here . . . we're safe.*

We're all about four seconds from eternity—four seconds from death, four seconds to life.

## That Chattering Echo

The night of the crash, my mind raced over the events of my life and I was overwhelmed. Even now, my eyes fill up as I think over the events that shaped me—what grace I received, this gift of unmerited favor in my life. I love to remember it, to meditate upon it. But it wasn't always that way. I used to fear being alone with my thoughts.

Sooner or later I found myself alone, with my thoughts chattering away at me. More often than not, there was no reply, just an echo. An echo in your head feels different from silence. It's recognition that no resolution has been formed. At least with silence you can close your eyes and fall asleep. With an echo you're forced to ask, *What's that sound? Why can't my thoughts and memories come to rest?* That was me. I realized that the echo I heard was evidence of emptiness, an emptiness amplified by the rattling of my own words: *Oh God, what am I doing?*

The echo was the sound of my pride when it's stripped of all its false values—in the corner of the brain realizing it's been had—like a blip on sonar. When I realized my very own pride had driven me to this place of emptiness, my soul clenched in anxiety.

That was me—afraid of the echo, driven to make sure I drowned it out with everything life could offer. I learned that if I kept life fast enough and fun enough and risky enough, I could blow through all the emptiness. But the echoes don't just go away. When the party ends, they come back—seeking revenge.

For me, in my twenties, crazy thoughts echoed in my brain. Thoughts of fear, *What if people discover the real me? Who is the real me?* Those echoes, those thoughts, haunted me. So I did my best to bury them and move on to the next kegger, the next girl, the next whatever.

But as I discovered, there's no contentment in burying thoughts of regret. Those seeds sprout right back and spread. Eventually you'll do anything for a solution—either you find a way out or go deeper into the muck. I went deeper and still deeper. It made sense. How stupid. People seem to want guys like me—son of a preacher man—to have some scandalous reason for all my "mistakes." But my scandal is less of what you might expect and more like something we all deal with: our dirty selves.

How can it be explained, this rebellious spirit welling up in a heart without excuse? Who could I blame? I didn't live a rebellious life because my father hurt me emotionally or because my parents neglected me for ministry life—thank God.

I didn't have some big wound that drove me over the edge; I had *Andrew*. Me. I was in love with myself. I wanted to be cool. I wanted the girls to like me. I wanted every cool guy from every cool clique to think I was cool so I could date the girls from that clique. But I felt people loved me for being that kind of person. It made me seem like I was no respecter of persons, open-minded and broadly accepting, and I fed on their love, their acceptance.

## Attention Grabber

Early on in life, I started pushing the envelope to gain attention, and I loved it. Fire was an easy attention grabber. And I liked to watch things burn. My friend Bailey and I were pyros. We loved to mix it up with fire. We'd make plans for days. Periodically we would drop a gallon jug of gasoline off the nearby overpass onto the open road and ignite it just for kicks. Initially our idea was that the flames would be significant, having no idea they'd rise up and nearly engulf our heads as we stood looking down.

Our actual plan was this: we'd wait for a single car's

headlights to peek out of the distance, and as the car rounded the corner we would light the gas—just enough to startle, but with no intention to hurt anyone, and certainly not close enough that they might actually be able to catch us. It was a dangerous prank, but that was our MO. Especially the not-getting-caught part.

The result we were looking for was the locking up of the brakes and the careening and fishtailing that would wave the headlights like a Hollywood opening, revealing for that briefest of moments the green Douglas-fir forest that lined the highway. Then the driver would regain control and pull over to determine what was blazing a mile ahead. People would drive up to the flames and flip out.

We created havoc and loved it. We did all of this to have a story to tell. We weren't the only ones looking for attention, but we were determined to be masters of it. And, good or bad, we stuck together through many more crazy adventures. Even to this day—forty years on—we're still at it, just looking for appropriate outlets at the moment.

We developed a little cohort of like-minded crazies, all wanting to crank things up with pranks, fast living, and general mayhem. We would fabricate fully clothed, life-sized dummies and hoist them over a hedge, down a little hill directly onto Walker Road in front of oncoming cars to hear them lock up the brakes and get a little chase going. But we knew all the forest paths *and* that we'd never get caught.

In a MacGyver sort of way, my childhood was one big weird science project. If we weren't igniting the road, we were figuring out the science to Molotov cocktails and how we could use them in our arsenal. Remember, we didn't have the Internet, so we'd find out on our own and use creativity—constantly engineering and scheming and figuring out through trial and error.

It never ended. Bailey and I, for example, would pull the bristles out of a rubber-cement jar and replace it with a wick. After we lit the wick, we'd throw it against the outside wall of the school gym. When the glass jar broke against the wall, rubber cement would spread all over and burn and burn, crackling and popping, thick black smoke and hot. We thought we were just having fun. We thought we were just pushing things a bit. Life was too boring without Molotov cocktails and rubber-cement bombs.

I easily justified all these inane activities. But this kind of living blossomed from ignorant adolescence to out-of-control deviance. The older I became, the more my time grew less and less positive.

Life, for me, progressed from boyhood adventurous innocence to something else. For years, we innocently engaged in building a zoo between our two houses. Over time we acquired hamsters, gerbils, mice, turtles, cats, birds, rabbits, a goat, chickens, aquariums, hermit crabs, frogs, lizards, and more. But somewhere along the way it became necessary to build in more excitement.

So, we progressed from building zoos to building explosives with match heads; eventually we'd try to build better pipe bombs or smoking devices for the express purpose of raising hell. Mom found our smoking devices on a couple of occasions, and even though she didn't know what it was, she knew it represented no good. She and Dad were wise to refuse to let it slide without challenge. I was good at not getting caught, but too often forced them into the position of using discipline to show me love. The borders they established were clear. When I crossed them and they called me out—from boyhood pranks to drinking and driving—they laid it down. I challenged their love with my disregard for it.

My parents never condoned my reckless choices. But when they enacted their rules or discipline I responded by becoming even more duplicitous. Even though they established borders, they also didn't go overboard. They struck a balance between giving me guidelines for life and knowing they couldn't change my heart. It's only now, parenting three children of my own, that I can appreciate the faith it took to release my heart to God.

When you're young, you have a built-in excuse mechanism for bad behavior. But what I didn't know then was that as I continued to make bad decisions, those decisions began to warp my mind and heart. My young life was formed by reckless fun and mayhem—all the while I fed off the attention and the popularity my actions garnered. I would do anything for acceptance, all under the guise of not caring what anyone thought.

⁜ ⁜ ⁜ ⁜ ⁜ ⁜ ⁜ ⁜ ⁜ ⁜ ⁜ ⁜ ⁜

Now, as I flip through the pages of my life, I find a string of these stories that seem unrelated. They're crazy stories, like the ones you just read, but they progress into a dark place— it was a time of my life I spent experimenting with how deep I could venture into drugs, girls, and alcohol.

These stories light up my memory like those old big-bulb multicolored Christmas lights that blink randomly in the weird neighbor's window. Those lights don't make a whole lot of sense when they're kept up all year—only when it's Christmas.

My stories feel like those lights, only having a sensible place when they're told in the context of the greater narrative that now rules my life. From those blinking-light stories this book emerges.

Over the months that this manuscript took shape, I began to see a distinct "guiding" element to it. Hindsight aids clarity. Like climbing a tree, which is something else we did a lot, you can survey all of life up to the present. The higher you ascend, limb by limb, the greater the perspective. All the while, the tree continues to grow. You can laugh at some actions. But in viewing others, you slink in closer to the trunk behind the boughs, hiding in complete embarrassment and regret.

Looking back, I see my restlessness. My spirit was always on the move. My mother tells me that I was like a frog living in two ponds. I didn't overtly hate God; I just didn't care. The world was my love. That restlessness ended up pushing me to places I never thought I would go. Those places, beneath the party-fun surface, were often dark and lonely; but for some strange reason they felt good to me. Like trying a cigarette for the first time—you know it isn't right and it burns your lungs, but the feeling you get from doing it keeps you coming back for more. But even though I ended up doing some crazy things in my youth and early adulthood, the rear view shows a providential hand watching over me all along the way.

This book, then, is a peek into my life, but more than that, it's a story arc that tells how a life that was discarded and broken can be gathered up again and remade. It latches on to the same ideas that even the ancients captured. The letter-writer, Saul of Tarsus (who later became Paul, an apostle of Christ), wrote on this idea and it is what I found to be true: humankind can never extend past the infinite reach of God's offer.

No matter how advantaged or disadvantaged, no matter how far from God we think we are . . . He is there and He calls out.

❊ ❊ ❊ ❊ ❊ ❊ ❊ ❊ ❊ ❊ ❊ ❊ ❊

Really, I was like anyone else—rattling and hearing echoes because I wanted to be loved. Wanted to be accepted. My great rebellion was just like the rest of the world's great rebellion. I couldn't get over me. My pride overwhelmed all possibility for lasting good. The great English writer Somerset Maugham captured what's true for all of us when he wrote, "If I set down every action in my life and every thought that has crossed my mind, the world would consider me a monster of depravity." Perhaps at some point in the coming pages you'll think me a monster. You'll be right. Monsters emerge out of the echoes—out of the absence of love, out of the absence of realizing that love is right there in front of them. And there I was, caught in the rebellion of pride, a monster who couldn't see love and acceptance for what it was.

Compound my drive for acceptance with the fact that I had no social filter, no spam catcher, so to speak, no governor that regulated the gas pedal of my life. I lived careening around at full throttle. It's how I've always been. And I liked being around individuals who pushed those same limits. When I think about life as a teenager and college student, I see how I surrounded myself with people of similar interests. That decision really defined much of my early life.

But, looking back, I really had no reason to live my life like one continuous "middle finger" at the world. What was my secret life? Was it something I didn't want people to see? Some of it was that. But my secret was also something I hid behind. I hoisted up a *me* I wanted everyone to see. I wanted people to see me as successful, good-looking, and adventure-some. But when I was alone and could let the facade down, the *me* staring me back in the face scared me. I wanted no part of it. Give me a party, some drugs, and my good times before you give me *the real me*.

There was no pain others could suffer, no matter how awkward and uncomfortable it got for me, that made it worth me stopping my way of life. If it paid dividends for me in terms of being the star of the party, I went for it. I remember one story that encapsulates just how selfishly I lived.

On my twenty-first birthday, spring break 1987 came early at the University of Oregon. My mom worked hard to keep the family close, so, in her incredible love for us kids, she generously arranged a ski trip to Whistler, Canada. This was a long drive north from school for me, maybe eight hours from Portland and ten hours for me from Eugene. She and Dad pulled in the goodwill of a number of family friends to make it happen because we couldn't afford this sort of trip outright. They borrowed a house for our family to use, while sacrificially saving to make the whole trip possible for everyone.

But back at school things were just getting juiced up. The frat brothers had no choice but to throw a raging "twenty-oner" bash for me. *I'd be up with the family in no time,* they promised. Well, the tequila and the lingering student body that had nowhere to go got the best of me and before I knew it, while most of the student body eventually vacated Eugene, I was on a four-day bender that went from bar to bar, party to party, house to house.

Back in the day at the Beta house we had one pay phone for over fifty live-ins and no cell phones. The big steel box hung in the entryway to the house and it had a heck of a ringer on it. On day four of my festivities, it became apparent that someone was trying to get through. That pay phone rang every other hour until finally somebody wandered over and picked up—probably a visitor because all the "bros" knew better than to be on the hook to find someone in the house by picking up.

It was Mom.

I was so oblivious to the reality of the situation that her tirade of questions caught me off guard. I am ashamed to say I was so pickled that my brain had jettisoned the parallel universe that was my family. This was one of the worst affronts I had ever committed; I was two days late for our family vacation—one she made great sacrifices to make happen.

She told me she would just cancel. I begged her not to, borrowed a car, and tore up there. The car ride with my family from Portland to Whistler was the most intense drive ever—the kind when your thoughts invade every nook and cranny of your mind; the kind when the wheel-hum and cabin noise produce a prison cell of silence that is really noise, the noise of guilt. I had embarrassed Mom beyond any reasonable excuse she might give to the family who owned the house we were borrowing. It was one of the most clear and direct pains and embarrassments I had caused her and Dad. Just blatant disregard for the hopes and dreams of those most dedicated to me for the most useless and damaging of short-term experiences.

꙰ ꙰ ꙰ ꙰ ꙰ ꙰ ꙰ ꙰ ꙰ ꙰ ꙰ ꙰ ꙰

We all have our secrets; we all have stories that mark our journey. As I reflect on the road I've traveled to get to where I am now, I weep. I could be dead by now or slumped somewhere in the south of France. I could be lost to my family or at least estranged—all of my own doing. But I'm not. And even as I write, I am struck with gratitude for the love of my folks and for the Divine hand that kept me safe and continues to make me whole.

※ ※ ※ ※ ※ ※ ※ ※ ※ ※ ※ ※ ※

Days after the plane crash I sat on the veranda under a vine-wrapped hardwood pergola with my wife's family, soaking in the Jamaican night sky, enjoying a huge meal. My stitched face was still bruised from slamming into the seat in front of me. My past gave me the eerie feeling that I got sucker-punched in a barroom brawl. That night, though, we celebrated life together and toasted to God's provision and to family—the morning found us carrying forward that feeling.

Jamaica is not all white sand beaches; the interior burgeons with beautiful rich countryside and high peaks. The next morning, we were headed up the stepladder Blue Mountain roads to a special little cottage tucked on the side of one of the peaks, amid the coffee fields. It was the very same cottage in which God confronted me sixteen years earlier in my life's most humbling and startling moment.

Everything seemed to be drawing me toward the next great thing God was teaching me. Reflecting on my past, the plane crash, staying in that special cottage—I felt God was saying, "In good times and in what seems like bad, if you have learned nothing else, realize that I am with you." Dad's mother, Grandma Palau, had a needlepoint hanging in her home that quoted a promise of God: "I have said these things to you, that in me you may have peace. In the world you will have tribulation. But take heart; I have overcome the world."[2]

As we drove up to the cottage I could hear God again saying, "Look, Andrew. I delivered you once way back when you thought you were too far gone. I delivered you and your family this time when all seemed like it was going so well. I am the delivering God—you are always in My care, in My love."

Some people think the horrible or destructive things they've done in the past cast them so far away from love and acceptance that those things determine who they are as a person. But that's not true. I'm proof. Others think that because life is going so well they don't need God. The plane crash taught me that's not true. I never want to be doing so well in life that I think I need no one—that I don't need God.

That night on the veranda we laughed and cried and shared our love with one another. The time was sweet, and the cool Jamaican air holding the sweet scent of the evening release of the ylang-ylang tree gave us an otherworldly feel. And in that time I was overwhelmed by the grace that continues to paint my life and family. I was also reminded of the mercy that peeks through the cracks of my life—

the plane crash. Mercy rested on my face for days in the bruises and cuts of the crash. And I am not one to take His mercy lightly.

In the film *Alive*, a Uruguayan rugby team's plane crashes in the Andes Mountains. Death seemed imminent, and they make horrific decisions in order to survive. Now, with some "food" and water, Ethan Hawke's character, Nando, says that as long as he has meat in his belly and legs to walk, he will not rest until he finds a way out of the wilderness.

Like Nando, if we are to survive, each of us must make our way out of the wilderness at some point in life. I feel that as long as I have breath—in light of my close brush with death—I can't rest until I tell everyone I can about my sporadic misfit life, the secret life of a fool that really is no secret at all. It's the reality that we all wrestle with—do we live for ourselves or is there a greater call on our lives?

Near the end of *Alive*, when it seems that Nando and his best friend can't continue in their search for rescue, Nando tells his beleaguered friend, who collapses in defeat, to look out over the vast wilderness. Then he says, "You know what it is that we have lived this long, the way that we have— these seventy days? That we climbed this mountain? You know what it is? It's impossible. And we did it. I'm proud to be a man on a day like this: alive. That I lived to see it. Take it in. Look, it's magnificent. It's God. And it'll carry us over every stone, I swear it."[3]

When I look out over the mountains in life I've yet to climb, the valleys I've yet to cross, I can see what Nando saw in *Alive*—that indescribable thing that urges, that draws us onward in life, even when we're at our lowest. I don't know why the plane crash wasn't much worse. I don't know why God decided to remake my life. All I can do is live thankfully, knowing that God is alongside me over every stone.

That's what God does. He walks with us over the mountains, through the valleys, and into the rescue land—a land that looks like love.

# THREE
# FIRELANE 3

There's a way of life that looks harmless enough; look again—it leads straight to hell. Sure, those people appear to be having a good time, but all that laughter will end in heartbreak.

—Proverbs 14:12-13 MSG

I LOVED MY LEGOS. I loved my brothers. And, being a Portlander, I loved my Blazers. Like any other kid I couldn't get enough of neighborhood football, hide and seek on the street, or our little Four-A club my brothers Kevin, Keith, and Steve and I started with the neighbor kids. I was in Boys' Brigade—a program for young boys at our church. I made derby cars and went to summer camp. I did it all;

everything an evangelist's boy is supposed to do. And I loved it all. I memorized Bible verses, went to missions conferences, attended church every Sunday, played sports every Saturday, and had fun like any other kid.

But for me the rebellious attitude set in early. I still have the note from Mrs. Holland in the first grade—the one that reads, "Andrew is a great boy, but he has been talking with a foul mouth. Pat, I know he knows better." I knew that note would crush my mom, but I had to shrug it off. Naturally, I acted as if I had no idea of the meaning of the words, and I wrangled with my mom concerning my broader usage of them.

That memory weighs on me now as I think about it. I think of my own children acting that way and wonder: *Why would they do that? Why did I do that?*

Impressing people. Normal, right? Sure, but I wanted it all the time. I gave no thought to my steps. Blundering along blindly. Each foot forward led to more decisions of the same. Decisions that would mark my life for the next two decades, setting a deep pattern down a sad and foolish path.

❂ ❂ ❂ ❂ ❂ ❂ ❂ ❂ ❂ ❂ ❂ ❂ ❂

A cul-de-sac childhood is what most parents want for their children: safe, secure, and out of the way of traffic. I didn't live in a cul-de-sac, but my life resembled the security of one—shielded from harm, open to love. I had no real reason to wander outside the paved security of my upbringing other than my insatiable desire to please the most important person in my life: me.

It didn't take long for me to wander away from my upbringing. When I reached junior high and high school, I lied about things we were doing. We'd go on ski trips with the youth group and sneak weed and flasks of liquor on the chairlift, and at night we'd see how far we could get with any "willing" girls. On the outside I was saying all the right things, thinking that people had no clue my heart was adrift.

I don't know where this insatiable desire to please others came from, but I know it drove me to act out. It wasn't enough for me to be thought of as okay. I wanted to be thought of as exceptional at whatever—be it partying, rebellion, or just acting crazy.

A girl in high school called me out once and told me I was a hypocrite. She saw me smiling to people's faces and smirking as they turned away. I thought she'd be an accomplice and that the joke between us against the others would curry favor. But she turned on me. Inside I was hurt and shocked. I didn't want to be viewed as a hypocrite. I *was*, actually, a hypocrite; I just didn't want anyone to call me on it. I wanted to show her that I could be a hypocrite and still be a good guy. I wanted to be able to make fun of the old lady in our church and get the girl. My behavior was not rational. I was a walking contradiction.

### Red-Blooded

High school. My old buddies and I were like any other red-blooded Americans. We shot BB guns at lights and threw pumpkins at mailboxes while driving at high speeds. We skinny-dipped. We made darts out of eraser heads and stick-pins and hunted birds with them.

We ripped off beer from the neighborhood garages and stole liquor out of our friends' parents' liquor cabinets—making noxious mixtures of hard alcohol. It never ended. We were wild and we were fun, and most of it seemed generally harmless. But eventually all the little "harmless" things add up. You build immunity to them. Going only so far isn't fun anymore. You have to push things. Build up some calluses. We pressed the line and stepped over the line. Once past that line, things lost their innocence. It's lost in a moment when you're confronted with a decision. Fear and trembling. *Do I take a hit of the joint being offered? I can't look weak. What do I do?*

And I'd do it. Expecting fire to drop from heaven and relieved to see, hey, it did not. Maybe I can get away with more than I've been led to believe. It was the beginning of a journey down a road that was fun in its season, no two ways about it, but would eventually lead to emptiness.

Once, my high school social studies class flew down to San Francisco from Portland to see a Michelangelo exhibit. My buddies and I bought a pipe and some dope from a guy at Fisherman's Wharf, bootlegged some beers and Bacardi, and hosted a party in one of the hotel rooms. We stayed under the radar as much as possible but took every opportunity to get wasted and create havoc, totally disregarding any rules or regulations for the trip.

The proverbial slippery slope got steeper and slipperier.

In one long stretch of high school, I was getting stoned three times a day: on the way to school, at lunch, and on the way home from school. It was in high school and early college that I really "pinned it," so to speak. I smoked hard and often. We were so obsessed with "taking hitties" that we hid bongs at every neighborhood park in Beaverton. We created names like "Nessie," "The Cube," and "The Wizard" for the secret bongs.

We created our own fun. We loved our pet bongs and were proud of our jungle parties too.

Jungle parties? you ask. Well, preparation for them was half the fun. After pounding down a few beers, we would drive our cars around town and the neighborhoods, peeling out in front lawns, ripping out ivy vines, rhododendrons, and small trees to use in creating the jungle. Depending on whose parents were out of town, we'd start a roaring party and decorate the inside of the house with the stolen vegetation to look like a jungle. To celebrate the theme, we made jungle juice, gallons of 151-proof rum and Hawaiian Punch mixed special for the party in thirty-gallon garbage cans. It made you wild—jungle wild. You can imagine the insanity that ensued. Those poor peoples' houses! You can be sure I was smart enough not to ever have one in our house.

Once, I and three of my closest friends—Justin, Tom, and of course, Bailey—bought four fifths of liquor: rum, vodka, tequila, and bourbon whiskey. We sat in my Honda in a wooded parking lot across the street from the high school. We knocked back a good number of straight shots before heading into the basketball game to see our friend

Eric Lautenbach play. Eric was our guy. We went to fire him up but couldn't really care less whether we won. If we did, though, we'd have even more reason to celebrate.

We needed a good lathering, however, before we showed up in front of our classmates and teachers. Thus, the parking-lot shots. To cap off our pregame warm-up, Bailey, who had been lagging behind, was charged to throw down some tequila, but he immediately threw it back up, all over the guys in the back seat. That was his sweet revenge, but he never lived it down. We chided him hard and often for his soft tummy. He would always retort, "My stomach just rejected it!"

So, we cleaned him up and went into the game.

Ridiculous how we thought no one knew how drunk we were. We thought we blended in with the crowd at the game. You know how it is at that age—sixteen trees on a half acre is "the woods" and you think that the gym is a massive raucous place you can get lost in. Remembering the scene now, it felt like we floated into the gym, that we were somehow on the outside looking in at all the unsuspecting folks hollering for a foul. We were like ghosts, like the outlaws in *Young Guns* who drank a mysterious concoction and thought they couldn't be seen as they galloped through the Indian graveyard.

We were normal and invisible all at once. We drank our concoction and walked through the graveyard in the high school gym. No one knew and no one could see us.

But of course, people knew.

Once our team won, I ran onto the court with the mob to congratulate my friend Eric. As I hugged him I felt a tap on my shoulder; strong hands whirled me around and hugged me tight. It was Mr. Al Egg. Al was one of the most respected men I knew. He led our school's huddle for Fellowship of Christian Athletes. Not that I attended FCA; I wasn't even an athlete. I would only show up if I knew there was a cute girl there. But Al was and is an upstanding and godly man who cared greatly for the young people in our school and community.

I turned to find Al standing in front of me, clutching my shoulders, his deep eyes filled with concern. If anyone had a reason to be concerned for me, it was Al. He and his wife had gone through the greatest challenge a parent can experience. His daughter had been in a drunk-driving accident a year earlier following a high school football game. After a week in a coma, she died. She was a junior. We all knew her. I tremble writing about it even now—how insensitive and flat-out disrespectful I was to him. Of all the people to see through my charade, he was the one willing to confront me; he was the only one that particular night.

"Andrew, you have to be careful. Please promise me you'll be careful, Andrew. *Please* . . . be careful. Please don't drive."

He looked into me.

"I will, I will. I'm not going to drive . . . *mumble, mumble, mumble* . . . " I tried to be serious. *Oh yeah, oh yeah. It's serious. Right?* I thought. I heaved lies into his face along with my liquor breath and turned to do more congratulating.

*I'm invisible. I'm normal. I'm serious. I'll be careful.*

But within the hour we were all back in the cars and we brought four younger guys along for the ride. They needed to get to a party, so everyone jammed into my Honda like circus clowns.

We headed up Cornell Road—prepared to pull a driving gag Tom and I had experimented with a few times. You take a right onto Leahy Road, which is a steep slope that hangs a huge hairpin to the left. But unbeknownst to most people, you can also cruise forward onto a virtually unseen road that drops out of view in the shadows.

You fake the left turn but stay straight to get air. It was nuts. We had frightened a couple of first-time unsuspecting passengers on it. We would fake argue about which way to go and then feign that we were losing control of the car. We'd fake the left-hand turn but let the momentum take us off the jump. It would freak people out.

On that night, the freshmen received a healthy dose of "the left turn."

"Ah, which way, Tom! Which way?" I yelled.

"Left here! Left here! Left here!" Tom yelled back.

"Here?"

The screeching tires, the yelling—it was complete mayhem in the car right up until we hit the jump. For a few seconds there was nothing, only the thrill of the jump and us feeding off the fear of the freshmen. We landed the jump and the young guys went into hysterics and cursed us up and down. It was epic.

Though our little trick worked, I continued to barrel through the neighborhood, forgetting momentarily that there were other corners to negotiate. The extra weight in the car caused me to lose control. We went sideways into the curb and onto someone's front yard, folding the tires underneath the chassis and totaling the car. This was a quiet neighborhood, like the one I live in now; our "minor" incident caused quite a stir.

We yelled at the freshmen to get out of the car.

"You guys beat it. You can walk to the party from here. You're only a mile away!"

They ran, dazed and scared. We, on the other hand, laughed about the whole thing—just par for the course. I managed to get the car started and backed it off the yard, but it wouldn't go any farther. We were near Wayne Jackson's house and thought about going there and calling someone about the car. But instead of dealing with it then, we decided to head over to the party.

We grabbed our liquor bottles and—*clank, clank, clank*—ran down the street laughing until we arrived at Tom's house. We jumped in his VW bus and headed to the party. I thought it was far better to deal with the accident in the morning. No sense ruining a good night for something that could be handled later.

Meanwhile, as we cranked things up at the party, the cops arrived on the scene of the accident. They began searching for the driver, thinking that the car might have been stolen and junked or that something tragic had happened. But nothing tragic had happened. Quite the contrary.

At 2 a.m. Wayne, whose family lived next door to the crash site, showed up at the party, saw me, and said, "Andrew, what are you doing? Don't you know that the cops are looking for you down where you guys left the car? And your mom is down there too, and they are giving her a hard time."

"What?"

"Yeah. They've got dogs out there, thinking that you guys might be hiding in the woods or something. You've got to deal with this."

I took a couple hours to sober up and tried to sneak into the house. But there was my mom, still awake, worried sick. Dad was on the road, so she had to deal with this on her own. She gave me the number of the officer who was at the scene. He gave me a ticket for hit-and-run driving—a felony charge. For hitting a bush? What was that officer thinking? I didn't care. In the innermost part of me, I was ashamed of hurting my mom; yet the story became a badge of honor and got told around the school for years.

⊞ ⊞ ⊞ ⊞ ⊞ ⊞ ⊞ ⊞ ⊞ ⊞ ⊞ ⊞ ⊞

I found Al Egg a few years back and apologized. I told him I was grateful that he had loved me enough to not let me squirm out of things without a confrontation. Al is a great family friend and still touches hundreds of lives for good year by year. I consider myself fortunate to be alive to thank him and to have him as a model that I can follow.

He has always infused himself into the lives of students. He's gifted like that. When I was drunk that night at the game, all I cared about was how much chaos I was going to create, but Al could see past that and recognize the potential inside of me. He was a blessing then, and he continues to bless.

When I stand back and look at the odd blinking Christmas lights that represent the stories of my life, I see people like Al Egg in those stories. Looking back affords me the opportunity to see things I didn't see before. People like Al Egg were ambassadors, acting in the name of God and for my good.

These were ambassadors of God in my life. A common thread of these messengers wove its way through my life—like my dad, who always took me on walks so he could speak into my life; or my mom, who cared and sacrificed so much to give us kids a great upbringing; or my wife, Wendy, who knew there was something inside of me worth pursuing. They were like ministering angels to me.

## Radioactive

My decisions seemed innocent enough. "Oh, Andrew will come out of it." But I didn't. I suppose I could have. Many people do. But I made conscious decisions to keep at it, to essentially perfect my own decadent way that I had chiseled out of thin air. It wasn't really thin air; it was something that grabbed hold of me and I allowed it because I liked it.

The flip is that I was the kid every parent wanted little Amy or Billy to hang out with. How? I was good at the mask. You know, the mask that sits on our dresser; the one we don when we don't really want people to know the person underneath—the real me or you.

Or maybe it was that my mask was just so good-looking— I mean, I looked like a great kid. Right? I was gregarious and positive and quick with the "Oh certainly, Ms. So-and-so, we'll be real careful."

That kind of behavior seemed innocent at the time. My friends and I weren't committing heinous crimes; we were just having fun. But as the proverbial line I was told never to cross continued to expand outward, I suddenly discovered that I was far from the expectations and hopes and dreams my parents and teachers had for me. In fact, those dreams and expectations stood so far in the distance that I hardly recognized them.

And what of my own expectations? What did I think I was going to do or who did I think I was going to become at this point in my life? The answer to that question is: I never gave it a thought. I was who I was at that exact moment in time. Doing shots in the car with the guys, driving like crazy people around the countryside, and lying to respectable adults along the way was all part of the "in the moment" state of mind I adopted.

In a way, I was always in that car throwing down shots and running into life half blind. The seemingly innocent things I was doing with pipe bombs—obviously not so innocent—and with match bombs and bongs, those were all seeds I was planting. I should have known, but never prepared for that future harvest. I had no idea that the seeds were radioactive.

## Firelane 3

Firelane 3 was one of the forest roads we partied on regularly. One night, my senior year, a bunch of us drove up for a bonfire and typical shenanigans. People from school drove up to hang—it was one of those nights when the crowd swelled . . . people were everywhere. A couple of us were messing around with a crazy-man mask—you have seen it before. It looks like Uncle Fester of TV's *The Addams Family* with a big gash on his forehead. I had it on for a time and was scaring other kids as they exited their cars along the forest path and made their way up the hill to the party. But I got bored after a while and took it off.

Then my friend Mark grabbed it and put it on. Poor Mark. Meanwhile, a big brute-of-a-junior had shown up in his truck and was yelling, "Where's Andrew Palau!" wanting to prove something. He was yelling obscenities and telling everyone in colorful language how he was going to tear me up.

To this day I have no idea what he wanted. I had no idea what I had done; after all, I was a lover, not a fighter. I still chalk the whole thing up to a junior-senior rivalry. So, I stood there by the fire with my head down, thinking, *Oh man, I'm dead.*

Someone told him how he could find me—I was the one wearing the Uncle Fester mask and scaring people. He didn't know Mark had the mask on now. The brute saw Mark stumbling up the trail wearing the mask and, thinking it was me, pummeled him. He knocked him on the ground and leveled punches to his face.

Poor Mark. Turns out he was a friend of this yahoo.

"What's going on?" he screamed. "What are you doing? It's me, Mark!"

Not one to miss an obvious cue to hightail it, I raced out of there.

░ ░ ░ ░ ░ ░ ░ ░ ░ ░ ░ ░ ░

A firelane is something intended for good. It's used to access the forest so rangers can extinguish fires should the need arise. But we used it to start fires in our lives—fires that we would one day have to extinguish, or have extinguished for us.

I was on a path that led to nowhere, using a firelane to get there.

# FOUR
# POURING GAS ON OPEN FLAMES

I've been putting out fire with gasoline.

—David Bowie

I GRADUATED FROM high school in 1984. I enrolled at Biola University, a Christian university based in La Mirada, California, but only lasted a year. They saw my interests were in other places. I spent more of my time hanging out at the beach, smoking, and attending punk rock concerts than on campus. They graciously allowed me to finish the year. From there I headed home to the University of Oregon in 1986.

I grew up loving the Ducks, so it was good to be home. By the time I arrived at U of O, I was out of control, as if my early-life idiocy wasn't enough. I ratcheted things up about ten notches. I became an incessant partier—the frat life didn't help my natural tendencies in this area. If anything, living in the frat house empowered me to be my most destructive self.

A frat brother of ours in college had an old VW Bug. We would rally it around and take it off-roading—hammer the daylights out of it. It was a thrasher Bug.

One lazy day, the car was sitting out behind our fraternity's parking lot. The old Bug had seen better days. No one had driven it for a couple semesters. Our boredom fed our deviant curiosity. "I wonder if it would catch on fire?" someone asked. Surely we could blow it up, we thought. I had seen it done on TV. So we made sure it had some gas left in it and Molotov-cocktailed it for a solid hour. But it never blew up. It just sat there and burned.

Finally, the fire department came and extinguished the blaze. It was no surprise to anyone that almost everyone living at the house was eventually kicked out, and the fraternity was banned from the university. If you walk up to a U of O graduate and mention the Beta House, which one typically does not do, he or she would know in an instant what you were talking about and look at you askance. Our frat was renowned for all the wrong reasons.

I had no problem pulling stunts like the "flaming Bug." I thrived on burning Bugs. It was around this time in my early college career that I began crafting my persona. The "I'm-a-lover-not-a-fighter slash do-anything" Andrew moved into a refining process. My penchant for lighting things on fire notwithstanding, the thing I lit up most in life was a cigarette. I smoked two packs a day. I loved to fire it up and brood, curse, heckle—or whatever. I was famous for having that boyish face framing that dangling cigarette. My buddies often recall, "Remember when we lived in the 'house of shade.' We would come in and Andrew, invited or not, was always there smoking his cigarettes." It's the me I wanted people to see. It was a me I thought I wanted to be.

I always had some Johnny Walker whiskey on hand. If we needed drugs, one of us in the house was sure to know how to procure the right stuff. College set me free—no one looking over my shoulder, no one to be accountable to. I took my new freedom by the neck and wrung the life out of it.

The lover-not-a-fighter in me slowly moved into the prolific category. There was something in me that knew it was wrong and hurtful to treat women as I did. I led them on. Lied to them. There was one span when I dated a girl from out of state while dating another girl from Portland over the summer. Then, back at school in Eugene there was another set of girls with whom I "hung out." My duplicitous nature was full of manipulation—I treated these people as my physical and emotional needs saw fit. I remembered how all of these things are described in the Bible as "acts that lead to death."[4] How rightly the Bible nails that truth.

I grew up reading the wisdom of Proverbs, but its insights didn't matter to me at that point in my life. I sought ways to get more involved with women even though I knew where that path would end.

The "me" I was refining and cultivating looked like an attractive person, especially in my world that prized that type of behavior.

## Self-Reliance

When I attended the University of Oregon, I majored in English literature. I fancied myself an intellectual. I read Blake and Kerouac, O'Connor and Hemingway, Conrad and Fitzgerald. I knew enough about literature to be dangerous. Knowing your way around a poem or a popular beatnik novel is invaluable when you're with the ladies (see comments above). But my romanticized persona coupled with my pseudo-intellectualism was just another veneer. I knew just enough about literature to sound like I knew what I was talking about to someone who doesn't. But I was a poseur.

Why would I do that? Well, to graduate from college for one thing. But also to look good for people and to project myself as this Hemingway type of character—masculine, sensitive, and brooding. I followed Hemingway's footsteps. When life became obtuse, he used a shot glass and a shotgun. I had my own tools.

Emerson, the famous writer and existential philosopher, wrote a classic essay titled "Self-Reliance." When I read it, I was drawn in by the brawny prose and was moved to exert myself into the world:

> Trust thyself: every heart vibrates to that iron string. Accept the place the divine providence has found for you, the society of your contemporaries, the connection of events. Great men have always done so, and confided themselves childlike to the genius of their age, betraying their perception that the absolutely trustworthy was seated at their heart, working through their hands, predominating in all their being. And we are now

men, and must accept in the highest mind the same transcendent destiny; and not minors and invalids in a protected corner, not cowards fleeing before a revolution, but guides, redeemers, and benefactors, obeying the Almighty effort, and advancing on Chaos and the Dark.[5]

Though I don't endorse all or even most of Emerson's thoughts in this essay now, in college one idea caught me.

"Nothing is at last sacred," wrote Emerson, "but the integrity of your own mind." The essayist's words here encouraged me to place a premium on my own thoughts, to pull up my bootstraps and take it upon myself to get it done—whatever it was. In some ways, Emerson was correct. We should be independent thinkers. I, for certain, wanted to be an independent thinker.

But the crowd repeatedly lured me to act like one of them. Even though I desired to be the greatest among them in terms of how crazy I could be, we all did basically the same things. There's nothing inherently special about imbibing stiff drink and roughhousing. Didn't I have my own mind? I should have had my own vision for my life? The tensions pulled me: don't listen to the crowd; be your own man.

But here's where trouble begins. When the only thing that matters is *me*. Who is he who rebels, but the one who flaunts supreme disregard for his family and fellow man, spurning their love and trust for the woe of the world; the single-minded rebel toasting Emerson while drinking himself off a cliff.

⸭ ⸭ ⸭ ⸭ ⸭ ⸭ ⸭ ⸭ ⸭ ⸭ ⸭ ⸭

The Jay-Z lyric "life starts when the church ends"[6] typifies my view of life and church and God at that time. Life stopped at the door and restarted on the way out each Sunday—and that one to four hours of church served as the bubble I floated in from birth until I left for college.

Once in college, however, the morals of others seeped into my Christian bubble, causing it to burst. In some ways I had always waited for my church bubble to burst so I could finally "live."

Life started when I woke up and ended when I passed out.

My buddies and I used to say that it was better in college to have been a hard-charging partier from early on, through high school. That way many of the tougher lessons are learned over time and not just in a massive flame-out of drugs, alcohol, and women in the freshman and sophomore years. We saw plenty of flameouts in Beta House. Nothing sadder than some poor fellow's parents showing up mid-year in the family wagon, dragging off the stereo system and futon—his tail between his legs on the way to rehab or wherever he was headed next. Maybe it was good for those guys; get it out of their system and head into life.

For me, though, this was a way of life I was determined to make work for the long haul. Not a flame-out, but one continuous burn.

⁂ ⁂ ⁂ ⁂ ⁂ ⁂ ⁂ ⁂ ⁂ ⁂ ⁂ ⁂ ⁂

After a year at U of O, my parents noticed how badly I was slipping. One day my dad called me and we "talked." He suggested I take a year off, maybe go to Europe and travel a bit. The experience would be rich, he said, and it would be good to get away from university life. Plus, it would serve as a foundation for my schoolwork and provide me with a fresh perspective.

Yes! The idea served my persona well. I wanted to be like Echo and the Bunnymen meets Frankie Goes to

Hollywood—world traveler, sophisticat with my dangling cigarette—and now I could.

So, I moved to Cardiff, Wales—a great city in the south of the United Kingdom, several hours directly west of London— for a year and worked in Allen and Alice Caron's high-fashion clothing store. The Carons were my parents' good friends. They were involved in church and helped my parents in their ministry work. Over the course of that friendship, my family made several trips across the UK and the Continent. Typically, we rented a larger van and traveled the countryside. The Carons were fun and generous. They had no children of their own but poured their love into us boys. Their impact on our lives was significant.

I wasn't there long when the romantic notion of establishing myself as a clothier overtook me. I thought I would work for them the rest of my life. The Carons insinuated, at least I thought they did, that because they didn't have children of their own I might someday be able to take over the store if I worked hard and earned that right.

That possibility floored me. It was a dream. I liked fashion and design. I liked Europe. It sounded almost too good to be true. But they were serious about it. It's amazing how that comment affected me. Later on, after my stint in the UK, that comment and my experience with the Carons in Cardiff were the primary reasons I pursued the retail industry in Boston. I had it all planned in my head. I thought to myself, *I'll get a job at a high-end retail store, work it for ten years, gain great experience, and move back to Cardiff and take over the Carons' clothing store.* But let's not get ahead of ourselves, as I did in making this plan.

I settled in to working at the shop and loved it. But after a couple months I got restless. So I planned an excursion to France with a couple of my buddies from the university, CL and Connor. I asked the Carons what they thought about the trip. They were reluctant, but they obliged.

## From Cardiff to Marseilles, and Back Again

I liked Connor from the first time I met him at U of O. He was a rambunctious fellow, showing up first day from California with a Mohawk. He was quite the punker early on before it was popular. Now he is a super laid-back dude. Life is full of fun irony.

Connor was privy to the finer nuances of thrasher culture, so I was proud to share my stories from LA and Black Flag concerts at the Pit. He was fired up when he discovered I'd be spending the year in the UK. His dad worked for Pan Am, so we promised each other we'd meet up across the pond and hitchhike around Europe. And that's exactly what happened.

He procured his tickets and I was waiting for him when he landed in London. Though his plane arrived early in the morning, we hit the pubs as soon as they opened, and then were sadly reminded that pubs close early on in the afternoon. That was good fortune, providing the window of time we needed to sober up and hop a train to the port city of Dover.

We stayed in hostels: very little money, no cell phones (they didn't exist then!), and no credit cards. Just the open road and us. From Dover, we took the overnight hovercraft—seriously. Six hours to Holland on a hovercraft with a nightclub. We drank all night and awoke on the floor next to the table.

We had one goal in Amsterdam: get hash. We stayed there a day and a half before we got bored. To me it was a looming type of city—dreary, depressing, and dark. After buying a few bricks at their famous hash houses, we hightailed it over to Paris, where we were to meet up with another Beta bro, our friend CL.

But CL didn't show up because he'd met a girl on the train ride over. His priorities were questionable, so naturally, he ditched us without a second thought. As we waited in Paris, our money was dwindled away on cheap wine, baguettes, and cheese. The weather was beautiful those days but our hostel was not, so we spent most of our time in the *Jardin des Tuileries*. This and the other parks were idyllic, so we lingered and daydreamed about what we might do next. For some ill-informed reason, we wanted to go down to Marseilles but didn't have enough cash for train tickets.

Our quandary was whether to stay in Paris and fritter away more time and money or venture out on little substance. Good fortune arrived that day at the hostel when we ran into a couple of twerpy Canadians who were on the tail end of a road trip similar to ours. They were okay guys, but we only took interest in them after we heard they were indeed on their way home and leaving in a couple days—so they'd have some time remaining on their Eurail passes. Connor and I began bragging, bamboozling them with crazy tales—trying to impress them. They wanted to go party with us, but we lost interest fast as they were being stingy about the idea of giving us their passes.

We headed out to look for some food.

Out on the streets, Connor and I took to approaching sandwich stands. If no one noticed us, we'd reach across the glass, grab a couple of sandwiches, and run. On this particular evening, mid-nab, we heard people yell out, "Hey! Stop! Thief!" An unusually persistent little chase ensued.

But we escaped and had a laugh about the close call. When we returned to our little pad, we ran into the Canadians who were happy to see us—and so proud to tell us they were the ones who had shouted and given chase. They had spotted us across the street and were coming over to see what we were doing just as we were making the snatch and grab. They took advantage of their good timing to heckle us. So, it was our Canadian-twerp friends who caused the whole ruckus. We thought that was funny—maybe these guys weren't so bad. When we returned to the hostel we began sharing more stories, back and forth.

They told us about the advantages of traveling around on the trains, and that the two of them were, in fact, leaving tomorrow. We told them of our plan to carry on south, but that we were on the edge cash-wise.

As we swapped stories, I became very determined. *Connor and I have to have those Eurail passes if we are ever going to reach Marseilles.* We turned on the charm, kept pumping them with cheap beer, and eventually convinced the guys to give us the passes.

We took our new "buddies" out on the town and partied hard. Later, toward the end of the night, they seemed to equivocate about their decision. One of them said to me, "We think these passes will be great keepsakes for us. Maybe we should hold on to them."

That would not do. So, we enacted our we-need-those-Eurail-passes strategy and kept ordering drink after drink, and once we broke out the hash they were completely gonzoed. We got them so plastered, keeping the passes was a cinch. At the end of the night we helped them back to the hostel where they made complete idiots of themselves, running up and down the halls in their underwear screaming and carrying on. Everyone in the hostel yelled at them until, finally, they passed out.

Our plan worked to perfection. We slept for a few hours, woke up at 4 a.m., grabbed our gear and their passes, headed to the train station, and boarded the train to the South of France.

I'm not sure what we were thinking, but I'm sure we had romantic notions of what Marseilles would be like. We envisioned it as a chic and elegant city off the southern coast. I think it was originally Adam's idea, and he had gotten it confused with Ibiza or something. It was anything but. Picture a stereotypical gnarly port town and you have Marseilles. No raves or the clubs we thought we'd find—just a damp sea-front. We had grown truly low on money, so we couldn't afford to rent a room. Since it was warm enough in the day-time, we decided we could sleep on the beach. We froze!

We lived like hobos, sleeping under a small sailboat to avoid the local cops who were spraying water on the beach-vagabonds in order to run them off. We were so miserable we began turning on each other like *Lord of the Flies*; we'd fight for sweaters that we stuffed with dirty clothes in order to make pillows and wrestle under the sailboat like mongrel street dogs.

On our second morning a proper French hobo, dressed in a three-piece suit, approached us. While bumming a ciga-rette, he told us that down the beach, under the suspended roadway among the massive rocks was a *clochard* village. We had ventured around there while jumping off the boulders into the sea the day before, so we knew what he meant.

The *clochard* village was an organized affair with tents and lean-tos of all sorts and sizes, paths allowing access in and through, and laundry hanging on cords. Now, according to this man, the transients in the little village were talking about Connor and me. They could not believe we slept on the beach the night before and were astounded that we were stupid enough to do it again. Our new friend warned us that if we were on the beach sleeping under a sailboat tonight, the other hobos were going to beat us up and take our stuff.

Having reached the end of our rope anyhow, it didn't take us long to come up with a plan to bow out of France. Each of us had already worked out the details in our own minds. It was easy for Connor to decide. He was to take the train to Paris and fly Pan Am first class back to Oregon—first class! Here we had just been slumming on the Marseille beach, our lives threatened by hobos, and now Connor was going to board a plane and fly first class back home. Unbelievable.

He'd hop the rail straight to De Gaulle International and fly home.

And me? After seeing him off I would take the train from the airport to Calais, where I planned to purchase my ticket for the ferry. Then it would be Dover to Cardiff by rail and I'd be home.

I was fired up. I had been through so many hassles the last couple of days and was uncomfortable and ached for a warm bed and a hot meal. I was running a thin margin, with only enough francs left aside for the slow boat across the channel. We had maintained the presence of mind to check our travel guide to see the price of the fare, and I had squirreled it away. It was a beautiful day, clear enough to see across the shortest distance from France to England. The White Cliffs of Dover shimmered and I felt things were going to be fine once I got over there.

Yet fine was to elude me. When I attempted to purchase my ticket, the clerk informed me that I didn't have enough money. Apparently, the travel guide that Connor and I were using, with all the train and ferry fees in it, was so old that the prices were off. I was short the cash I needed to get across. The ship was just there, across the velvet ropes and down the gangplank! So close, I could almost touch it.

I pleaded with the clerk to let me on board. I showed her my Eurail pass—all I needed was to get over to Dover and I would be on my way home to my concerned family. But she wasn't having it. I don't think she understood a word of my plea. What was I going to do? There I was, trafficking my cube of hash over European borders. I had half a pack of Marlboros and my Johnny Walker scotch jammed in my bag of damp sweaters and crusty jeans. I was a sight to behold. Meanwhile, my best friend was yucking it up with the first-class folks over the Atlantic.

I was panicked. I was fired up. And I was not going to be stuck in Calais, France. This would not do.

There it was. Next to the ticket booth was the roped-off line for passengers to walk through, which led down onto the gangplank where passengers would board the ship. This was no Puget Sound puddle-hopping ferry. This was a massive cruise liner with multiple decks for cars and trucks and huge gathering areas throughout for people to sit and mill around and buy meals and beverages. If I could only get over there.

In a split second, I bolted.

Jumped the line and ran across the gangplank, past the guard and onto the ship.

Now I was a stowaway. Twenty-seven francs short and it comes to this. A small chiming alarm signaled and more guards began to cluster to see what the commotion was about. I hustled to the area where people were seated for their passage—the scene was similar to what you see at an airport departure gate. I jumped over a few seats and plopped down amid a startled family with older kids and tried to act normally. I tried to blend in and look like part of the family; maybe the guards would pass me by. And they did. People around me stared at me and whispered and shot me *What's your deal?* glances. A fair exchange for the moment of camouflage.

So, the chase was over. The delay was short. I thought I was safe. The boat pulled away from the dock and we began the 34 km journey (about 21 miles) across the channel to Dover. *Good times ahead*, I thought. But I failed to realize how serious this breach was to the captain and the company. Although it was pre-9/11, the international border crossing laws still carried weight.

The guards began a sweep of the entire ship. They were determined that in the hour and ten minutes they had, they'd find me. I moved from place to place, doubling back, hoping they would finally give up. But they didn't.

I was doomed.

If they didn't find me now, they would upon disembarking. They had me in a funnel. Plus, I had to consider passport control and customs. They had me.

The captain's quarters were a few floors below on a mezzanine level. I found it and knocked. The door opened and before me stood a beast of a man. He was the captain. This burly Norwegian stared at me and asked what I wanted.

"I want to turn myself in," I said. "I'm the one the guards have been chasing."

He looked at me, half tilting his beastly head like a Burmese Mountain dog, and laughed.

But the belly laugh lasted only a few seconds. After he gathered himself, he took a more serious posture.

"How much money do you have?"

I commenced telling him my woeful sob story. He must have thought I was just a pathetic traveler who was making up stories.

"Really, Captain, I didn't want to or plan to stow away. I just miscalculated the ticket and didn't have enough money. I panicked and ran on board."

I believed that after hearing my story he would have some kind of pity on me and perhaps take twenty francs and leave me a couple for lunch or something. Yes, I was naïve. He took all my money and reprimanded me and sat me in a little section of the ship—sequestered off by myself—until the ship reached port. He then proceeded to kick me off the ship with another reprimand. I was relieved. My fears had reached the obvious possibility that I could be jailed, and what if they searched and found the drugs in my hatband? Seriously? My hatband?

What a nightmare.

Yet somehow I was on my way again. I said to myself, "Now I'm home free. I can hop the train from Dover to London and then from London to Cardiff and I'm home."

I cozied up in a seat in the smoking car, lit a Marlboro,

and sipped a little scotch. I raised my pass, pinched nonchalantly between my pointer and middle fingers as the ticket-taker walked by. I handed him my pass, not giving it a second thought.

"Sorry, mate."

"Huh?"

"This is no good here," he said.

"What? I've been using this pass all over Europe."

"Sorry, fella. You can use this in France and the Continent, Ireland and Scotland and even Wales, but it says right here on the back that you can't use it in England."

I was stunned. Why not England? How could I even get to Scotland or Wales to use it if I couldn't use it in England?

I pleaded my case with him, hoping—praying—he would extend some mercy. But he didn't budge.

"I'm sorry, but you're going to have to get off."

I didn't go quietly. We kept at our bickering until he physically escorted me off the train, shoving me with a great huff to the platform.

Now completely out of money and with no mode of transportation, I had no choice but to hitchhike, which in England is tough. It's not like in the States where you can make a go of it if that's all you have to rely on.

I positioned myself near a high-traffic area where the ships were offloading onto trucks, hoping to score a ride. Finally, a kind trucker stopped, but he only drove me a short clip. After the trucker, I landed several little rides—almost from exit to exit—experiencing a breadth of characters.

Two young guys picked me up in their van. They were enigmatic fellows who didn't speak English. Eastern European. Judging by the interior decor of their van, they were into auto racing. These Frick and Frack characters gave me a weird vibe. I was happy for the short ride but was even happier when they let me out. I could imagine myself all laced up in the back of their van being taken to a speedway and used for a pylon—or shipped off to their mother ship waiting in another quadrant. My imagination was my filter on this occasion.

"Thanks for the ride!" *I hope I never see you weirdos again.*

I was getting weary and more hesitant about each ride as daylight began to wane. *What I wouldn't give to be able to sit down for a while and catch up with my thoughts*, I said to myself. But there was nowhere to go on these stretches of road.

If I could somehow reach the west side of London, I knew there was a hotel near Heathrow Airport where I had stayed with my folks on a number of occasions. *Perhaps I could figure out a way to stay there,* I thought. *If I could work my way around the M25 to where it connects with the M4 by nightfall, I could probably hole up in the lobby for a while.*

*Great, now I'm talking to myself.*

I finally reached the hotel just as the sun was setting. I milled around in the lobby swiping the finger sandwiches that people left behind. I planned to find a little nook where I could curl up for the night. The lobby was so massive I was confident there was no way anyone would notice me.

Before I bedded down for the night, I visited a wedding reception in one of the ballrooms. I stole more food and drank some champagne. Someone at the reception finally asked me what I was doing and whether I was friend of the bride or the groom. I made up a story about knowing John.

"I'm here with John."

"Who's John?"

"He's a friend of mine who . . . *murmur, murmur, murmur.*"

I bolted out of the reception and back to my little corner of the lobby as he went off to find security. Soon thereafter, the hotel staff became suspicious that I was crashing in their lobby. I tried to lie and tell them I was meeting my parents. And they actually felt conscientious enough to check out my story. They checked their lists to see if a mistake had been made. I pretended to be making phone calls from the pay phone. Finally, after 1 a.m. they confronted me. They caught me in my lie and threw me out.

Lucky for me I grabbed a few newspapers when I was stealing food and stuffed them into my bag. Those papers ended up serving as my bed covers. Not one to be totally defeated, I scoped out the back of the hotel to see if I could find a warm place to bed down for the night. In the rear of the hotel, near what I reckoned was the back entrance to the kitchen, was a large concrete pad with a massive vent jutting out of the back wall pumping out warm air. *Perfect*, I thought. *I can at least sleep in a warm place tonight.*

After I made my newspaper bed, I stretched out and shut my eyes. The hum of the vent lulled me to sleep.

Bang!

The kitchen door burst open and two busboys came barreling at me screaming obscenities in Urdu, intent on using some kind of violence on me.

"You vagrant! You can't sleep here! Get out!"

I was still half asleep but managed to gather my things and avoid a beat down. When I reached a safe distance, the busboys returned inside, laughing it up. I was so mad! *They probably just happened to come upon me back there—maybe they even came out by accident,* I thought. So I wandered back and set my bed up again, thinking, *That couldn't possibly happen again. They'll never think I'd come back after that.* Clearly, I must have been delusional and in desperate need of sleep. Just as I was about to settle down, the Pakistani busboys came at me again, this time laughing their heads off and hurling profanities at me. They came at me with pans of water ready to douse me.

They must have been waiting for me. It was like a game to them. It was so strange they could get the jump on me like that. But as I thought more on it I realized that along the entire breadth of the hotel wall was a row of huge black windows to the right and to the left of what I thought was the kitchen door. But what was actually behind that wall and the black windows was the bar. So everyone at the bar had a late-night front-row seat to my humiliation.

I had had enough. I walked down the road searching for a place to sleep. In the center of the massive roundabout was a little wooded area. It was cold and damp. But there were no Pakistani busboys with pans of water. I ignored all I had learned about the science of alcohol and its effects on body temperature and sipped Johnnie Walker until I fell into a fitful sleep.

I awoke as an English popsicle at 5:30 a.m. I thought it would be another long day of short hops, but to my happy surprise, the first person to stop for me was a compassionate military man. I told him my story and he offered to drop me at my house. I was amazed and grateful. My odyssey of sleeping on trains, under boats, and in roundabouts, as well as being chased by armed guards, Canadian twerps, Norwegian captains, and pan-bearing Pakistanis, was over for this American cowboy.

▒ ▒ ▒ ▒ ▒ ▒ ▒ ▒ ▒ ▒ ▒ ▒ ▒

Experiences like this shape us. In some cases, they even vault us onto another path entirely. As a twenty-year-old adrift in England, I imbibed whatever life presented to me, though often at great risk. While my do-anything mentality serves me well now in my vocation, there was a long stretch of time where it simply drove me into despair and introduced me to trouble.

### Back at Cardiff

When I returned, I worked day after day six days a week at the clothing store. I became bored, but I dedicated myself to settling down and taking advantage of this time to just chill and work. I didn't want to stress out my gracious hosts who had done so much for my family and me. I respected them and wanted them to think I was respectable. But my little French excursion had already made them wary.

So I kept things low-key. I lived above the shop and kept my wanderings to staying up late while polishing off a half dozen pints of lager, passing out, and sleeping in on Sunday. I would also wander down the street to Roath Park, a massive 130-acre park that surrounded a man-made lake. It's a stunning park.

I built some relationships in the community. The Ferraris owned a quaint café next door. I'd buy my coffee there some mornings. Every day I had lunch at the tandoori across the street and chatted with the owners. I also spent time with some teenage ruffians who hung out at this end of the park. They'd make fun of my accent and my Jack Purcells and Portland Trailblazers hoodie. They were nice enough—seemed more bark than bite. They moved in their little pack and skated most of the time.

Then I had also met this middle-aged man—maybe he was fiftyish—who seemed like a great guy. He took an interest in me, had a brother in America. I enjoyed our little chats about the culture and music and whatnot. I liked becoming more familiar with the local happenings. He owned a small business and gushed about his great wife and two kids. One afternoon he asked me if I wanted to go see a band at one of the pubs downtown. I asked Mr. Caron if he thought it was cool to go with him. He was visibly hesitant but agreed to let me go.

So, we made our plans. I met him down at the park; we grabbed a cab and headed for town. We hit several pubs and everyone seemed to know this guy, but I thought that was part of the pub scene—I thought this guy was just the popular "Joe" businessman. Still, I decided that I wouldn't get pie-faced on this first night out—more of a safety precaution than anything. We ended up at a quiet pub, dug into a new conversation, and had another pint.

As we talked, though, I felt strange. The room spun. I felt like I was getting sick. I knew I wasn't drunk; I had only had a couple beers. I should have been fine. I had to use the table to balance myself at some point during the conversation. I held on to the edge just to stay upright.

Finally, he said, "Let's go home."

I was so thankful. I felt awful.

"Yeah, let's go home."

"No, Andrew, I want you to go home with me, back to my place."

I didn't care where we went. I was spinning and needed to get out.

"Sure," I said. "Let's go back to your place."

Then, he clarified his intentions. "No, Andrew, I want you to go home with me . . . to sleep with me."

In a split second my mind cleared. I snapped upright, realizing that this whole thing was a ruse to get me into bed. Apparently, he had a buddy at one of the bars slip something into my beer—some drug to loosen me up, even incapacitate me.

I confronted him as best I could. "Oh no, man. You've got it all wrong. I'm not into that sort of thing."

"How do you know if you haven't tried it?"

I was adamant. "I'm not going home with you."

Then he became agitated and a little aggressive. We got into it verbally.

"You led me on this whole time. You knew what was going on!"

"No, no, no, you just got it all wrong. No hard feelings. Just drop it!"

Things got heated and I thought, *It's make or break time, and I gotta make a break for it.* I leaned forward, pushing heavily on the table, and used the leverage to stand up. The inertia helped me lurch to the right, and my momentum took me about fifteen steps to where the bartender lady stood, annoyed that I was stumbling across her bar.

"Can I help you?"

"Yeah, I need a taxi."

She helped me get a taxi and got my address to the driver. I flopped into the cab and passed out.

The driver woke me—annoyed that I had passed out in the back seat. I somehow paid him and he deposited me on the corner of Wellfield Road and Roath Park. It was a Saturday night after midnight, and the park was alive. Many of the people were shady characters. But I didn't care. I was happy to be away from the businessman.

I started feeling better and made my way up the three blocks back to the shop—back home. As I approached the edge of the park, I noticed a group of people, teenagers and older. Most of them were skinheads, and scattered amongst them were the ruffians I knew. I tried to make eye contact with them but we didn't connect. They recognized me but were not about to admit that to their older compatriots. About a block down, the gathering began to loosely line up across the road.

"Are you serious? You're really going to do this?"

Their intentions were clear. I was prime meat for a nice beat down.

*Can this night get any worse?*

My mind raced to concoct a plan. I knew if I could make it a few steps further down toward the punks, there was the alleyway to my right, then at the next left I would be in the alley behind the Carons' shop. Wellfield Road was littered with coffee shops and chemist shops—all kinds of little merchant shops. But behind the main road of storefronts were small alleys for loading access. I only had to make it down the alley to my right. That would give me a chance to reach the back of the Carons'. Then I'd hop the stone wall and be home free. I knew where the hidden key was—once found I would be out of trouble.

I lifted my head to look at the guys, made eye contact, then bolted down the alley, hooked a left, hopped the wall, and hunkered down. They exploded after me, the enthusiasm of the chase audibly rising. I could hear the clump-clump of their boots coming.

But I had made a mistake. I hopped the wrong wall. I had hopped the wall for Ferrari's, the café next door. I didn't move.

I waited the whole thing out. After about thirty or forty minutes of cussing and persistent searching for me, they tired and left. I climbed over the fence and into the rear of the Carons' shop. But the key was gone! I would have to walk around to the front of the shop and wake up the Carons in order to get inside. I worried my buddies would be waiting around up on Wellfield Road, so I waited a while longer and crept along in the shadows. Once at the front door, I rang the bell. Mr. Caron came down the stairs in his bathrobe. He unlocked the door, clank-clank-clank. I fell into the house on my side. Mr. Caron was astonished and indignant.

"You're drunk!"

"No, no! I'm not drunk!"

"How could you be so irresponsible?"

"No, no it was that guy—the businessman! He slipped me something in my drink. He drugged me."

I tried to tell him the whole story but failed miserably. Finally, he told me to just go to bed. But they stayed up and discussed things.

In the morning, they confronted me and asked me to tell

them exactly what happened. So, I divulged the whole story. The guy making passes at me, the gang chasing me, all of it.

## Enough Is Enough

My shenanigans surprised the Carons; they didn't know how to handle it. They didn't know how to handle me. I could tell the French excursion had affected their confidence in me, but the situation with the skinheads and the businessman elevated things so much, they were afraid to have me in the shop.

"Look, Andrew," said Mr. Caron. "This is unacceptable. We can't have either that man or those kids messing around knowing you're staying here above the shop. If you want, you can go home."

I didn't want to hear that option.

"Or, you can go to Bangor, Northern Ireland, and live with my sister and brother-in-law. They have a furniture store and you can do the same thing there as you're doing here. At least there you'll be safe from the people you're tangled up with here."

I was embarrassed. But I shrugged it off.

"Oh, okay," I said. "I'll go up there."

I headed to Bangor and started working in the Griffeths' shop. Brian and Thelma Griffeth were salt-of-the-earth people. Their children were bright and pleasant to me, generous just like the Carons. I would spend a week in the shop selling, followed by a week in the warehouse and on the delivery trucks. Then I'd continue to alternate. That was a rich time—lots more smoking and grainy stories from the guys about The Troubles, the conflict in Northern Ireland. I learned a lot. The Griffeths were serious churchgoers and had no clue about the extent to which I had walked away from my family's faith. They thought I was a chip off the ole block. So, of course they should ask me to speak to their youth group.

A youth group? Huh? What would I say to them?

I wanted to laugh and cry at the same time. Every part of that idea bugged me. I hated speaking in front of people. A healthy part of me feared it—I feared deliberately posing to know God in an intimate way yet living the way I did. I guess real Christian hypocrisy, to me, felt different than the other kind where people develop their own perception of you based on your dad or something and they see you doing crazy things. Like my high school days—I didn't pretend to be some great Christian kid following in my dad's footsteps. I was nice and kind when I needed to be but made no pretense about what I was about. I didn't care about that kind of hypocrisy because I wasn't posing as a Christian do-gooder. I just didn't care. In my mind, that was different.

I declined their invitation but they persisted. I declined again. They persisted.

"You don't need to *speak* to them like a pastor or any-thing, just let them interview you and have a conversation with them."

I didn't like this idea but I finally acquiesced. You can imagine my discomfort throughout the duration of the inter-view. My pits gushed. My eyes darted here and there. The kids asked me questions; the adults looked on. They were a conservative group too, so I didn't want to mess things up and say something stupid. It was awful, but I guess I made it through.

During the interview I was as honest as I could be with-out shattering their perception of me. Afterward I was grateful that the leader told me how much they appreciated my answers and being open about my uncertainties—which apparently they interpreted as the fear of God. You're darn right I feared God. But not exactly as they meant it.

Word travels fast. The report of my little speaking gig made it back to my dad. He and Mom were planning on coming to Bangor later in the month. He had just written me a letter to say how much he loved me and to share his love for God with me. You can see his effort in the lines of the letter—the heart of a father for his son laid out. But just before he sent it off, he heard this story of me sharing at a youth group and he almost withheld it. I am grateful he did not. The letter acted as a powerful seed planted in my life, and now I can read it and see Dad's consistent love, hopes, and expectations for me. What an example.

I treasure this letter. Here's what he wrote:

*Monday, 2:30 p.m.*

*Andrew,*

*Just hung up from our conversation regarding Mom's and my arrival later this month. So glad you gave a word to the teens on Sunday. I almost felt like not sending this enclosed letter after hearing that, but I hope you'll read it with my deep love for you in Jesus as your dad. Can't wait to see you soon.*

*November 1, 1986*

*Dear Andrew,*

*It was so comforting for me to talk to you over the phone from London to Bangor. Counting down! I wish we could have been out in London together and talked for hours but it did not work out. Also, I had wanted to write you—I'm as lazy as you. This is not the kind of letter you dictate to your secretary. It's family.*

*Mom and I are eager to see you this month. We miss you and love you a lot. So do the boys here at home. Andrew, I also wanted to write you since we didn't get a chance to walk and talk in London.*

*There's a phrase that keeps coming back to me every time I pray for you and think about you (and I do that very much as you can imagine—you are a son I love very much). When I was twenty-one like you, I took this little phrase for myself as I read the Bible with my buddies. It is: "But you man of God . . ." 1 Timothy 6:11. You were born, Andrew, to be a man of God. That's what God has for you. That is God's purpose for your life. Ever since you were a little boy I have had that expectation. Either on the phone or by letter, I can't remember now, the day I called Grandma Scofield from Cali, Colombia, she herself said similar words to me. The Lord God loves you with an everlasting love, Andrew. The first step he has taken to bring you to himself is that he went willingly and personally for you to a cross. On that cross, he became your substitute. He took your place and your punishment and forever removed your guilt.* "Christ died for us."

I pray that first of all, Andrew, that you would open your heart to Jesus Christ for sure. The day I prayed and asked Christ to give me eternal life a counselor used Romans 10:9–10 with me. He personalized it just for me. I've never asked you, Andrew . . . have you ever asked him personally?

"If you confess with your lips, Andrew, that Jesus is Lord and believe in your heart, Andrew, that God raised Jesus from the dead, you, Andrew, shall be saved. For it is with your heart, Andrew, that you believe and are justified and it is with your mouth that you confess, Andrew, and are saved." Then he closes verse 13 with this clincher: "For everyone who calls on the name of the Lord will be saved."

If you haven't made that decision for sure, Andrew, and if you want me to help pray with you—and nothing would give me greater joy in the whole world—I would do it . . . if you want. Secondly, a little phrase came to me a short while ago: The secret life is the secret. What you are in your soul, is what you really are. As a man thinks in his heart, so he is, says the book of Proverbs in the Bible. You will become a man of God, Andrew, when you specifically and clearly invite Christ into your soul.

You develop your inner secret life with your heavenly Father . . . on your knees reading God's Word . . . on your knees talking to God in prayer . . . on your knees singing and praising God . . . committed to obedience— whatever the cost . . . obedience even unto the point of death. Revelation 2:10 says, "Be faithful unto death, and I will give you the crown of life," Jesus promises.

Andrew, my love for you as my son is very deep. The potential I see in your life as God has made you is superb. You could bless and change and bring great happiness and eternal life to millions if you obey Jesus Christ as your Master and Lord. "Follow me and I will make you fishers of men." I took that quote from Jesus very seriously at your age. I love it. It's the best life in *the world. You will enjoy it too, my son, if you follow Jesus with all your heart and soul. What else is there in this rebellious world? Not much.*

*See you soon. I love you and pray for you.*

*Dad*
*PS: Read 2 Timothy 2:1–6 in the NIV.*

▓ ▓ ▓ ▓ ▓ ▓ ▓ ▓ ▓ ▓ ▓ ▓ ▓

Grandma Scofield made a prophetic statement when I was born. And Grandma is not notably prone to that sort of thing. She doesn't say things willy-nilly. But when Dad called and told her that I was born she told him, "Luis, this one is going to be an evangelist."

Dad knew exactly how to take that; he held on to it—stowed it away in his heart. He would share that story with me periodically when I was nowhere near walking with God, even resistant to it. Almost like he was reminding me of my destiny. I suppose when he caught wind of my little speaking engagement with the youth group in Bangor something perked up in his spirit.

Funny how you can find strands of your destiny in your memory when you take the time to search it.

Those walks Dad and I took were common for me growing up. When you're a young boy, it's tough to not feel awkward and squirmy, wanting such times to be over. But I did hear my dad's words of encouragement and correction. They stuck with me throughout my life.

I guess God enjoyed using my dad, and my mom, as He pursued me. He gave me every chance to come to Him. And though I ignored Him, He was faithful, and my parents were faithful. All the walks, all the letters, all the books Dad would send me with personal notes scribbled on the inside flap—all of it chipped away at my stony, rebellious exterior.

And as those who loved me chipped away, I lay beneath, deaf and foolish, refusing the hand outstretched to me.

*Rise, clasp My hand, and come!*
*Ah, fondest, blindest, weakest,*
*I am He whom thou seekest![7]*

## FIVE
# BELL IN HAND

In the days of my youth, I was told what it means
    to be a man. . . .
No matter how I try, I find my way into the same old jam.

—Led Zeppelin


**AFTER MY EUROPEAN** excursions and a return to U of O for my degree, I moved to Boston to pursue a career in retail. I chose Boston for several reasons, but mainly because it was on the other side of the country. It was time for a new path. My lifestyle transitioned into a grown-up version of my junior-high self. No, I didn't continue experimenting with gasoline and fire and handmade bombs. The experimentation was different, though equally flammable.

Outwardly I was doing okay. I had my university degree and lived in one of the premier American cities working my way up the corporate ladder. I maintained my self-centeredness and self-gratifying relationships. Though I dialed back a bit on the partying and drug life, I still lived as if God did not exist.

I was no longer a boy in college able to contrive excuses for my carousing. I was a man who chose to walk away from God. Far worse. Now I was grown up, but still obstinate. I kept my life together and managed to stay out of jail and real rock-bottom stuff, for the most part . . . outwardly anyway.

My internal narrative read much differently.

As time passed, I began to recognize the emptiness in my life. I began to feel a real sense of loneliness even though I had a great family and all the friends in the world. I was the ironic soul who stood surrounded by people, yet inwardly carried the burden of despair. Something was missing. *What am I doing with my life?* I thought.

This question vexed me. Even though I wanted everybody to think I was doing great, my inward existence seemed futile and embarrassing. Working up the corporate ladder was a farfetched statement. Reality? I was trying to make my way in life, doing the best I could. But despondency sank into me like a subtle virus—it latched on and infected other areas of my life.

But was I so surprised?

I had built my life on structures of glass—gleaming and sparkly but easily shattered with a pebble. I was trapped by all the things I had done in the past. The things that started out as "fun" and "exciting" now contributed to my unraveling. I could choose dozens of examples of how things began to unravel, but I'll stick with one. It's an obvious one: alcohol.

I abused it in this way. At first, I drank for fun, for social reasons, but in the end it was a trap. Anxiety was one of the primary reasons I began abusing alcohol. I couldn't go to bed sober with my thoughts. Whenever I found myself in that position—sober, lying in my bed, in the darkness of the night—all the garbage of my life flooded my mind and my heart. I'd lie there restlessly and think about all the people I'd hurt and all the lies I'd told, all of my cheating and stealing, the abusive relationships, my addictions, my arrogance and pride, and so much more would flood in.

I was like a prisoner caged in my thoughts, the guilt pressing in on me, overwhelming my spirit. I could not take it.

So, to avoid that situation, I found people to party with every night of the week, which wasn't too hard. But sometimes

I couldn't find anyone, so I'd end up riding the train, then the bus, to my apartment, and sitting alone on my couch, drinking beers and watching baseball into the wee hours of the night. On the East Coast you can watch West Coast baseball games until one or two in the morning. Eventually I would pass out on the couch and the TV station would sign off for the broadcast day. No twenty-four-hour cable back then. The screen would turn to fuzz. I'd wake up, turn it off, crawl into bed, hear the alarm, get up, and go to work in the morning. Then out partying. On and on it went. I wondered if, at some point, I would turn to fuzz and be shut off.

This terrible cycle continued in my life; it was my way of avoiding the reality before me.

I stepped right into the fool's world.

With an incredible display of imprudence and lack of wisdom, I had played this role in high school and college and now as an "adult." I was the fool. A fool is a silly person. I'd read enough to know the role, and I thought warmly of the court jester—the one who plays the clown to entertain all the people of wealth and influence. I was like a clown walking the tightrope, balancing plates and balls on my nose while whistling calliope tunes—the circus jester entertaining the folks who would look in on my traveling fair.

I went to great lengths to apply my makeup *just right*. I lived with a painted veil over my life that seemed more fun, more daring, more everything. I felt better for having a great fool's mask. I loved walking the tightrope, singing my silly songs. The safety net was below; I knew I'd be fine if I fell.

And I did fall. In doing so, I learned that fine is relative. Sure, I'd pick up the pieces, but then I'd find myself quickly wondering, *What's next?* Being alone and adrift, growing estranged from friends and family, began to feel less and less fine. If fine was the act of "getting by," I didn't desire to be fine. I wanted glory and love and power. Modern media mirrored my desires: sex and food and plenty of it. I wanted to rise above the mundane and indulge in the rich things in life, the things that made me feel good—that made me feel invincible.

When I fell from my tightrope all my plates and balls shattered and scattered. My mask smeared. My back hurt. My pride hurt. My heart hurt. When I looked around to see what the crowd thought, the stands were empty, no applause. *But I was told that the crowd loved when the clowns fell. What about the cheers and the laughs? What about the approval of man?* The fool was fooled.

## A Sobering Gateway

"You're a believer."

"What are you talking about?"

"You're a believer. Right?"

I didn't know what he was talking about. I was in a club in downtown Boston. The lights and the music pulsed. I was three thousand miles from my family and anyone who really knew my background. How did this guy know me?

"You're a believer."

"Yeah," I said hesitantly. "I am." Oh boy, I need to just cut this discussion short and scram. But part of me liked what he was intimating—that we were connected through a spiritual brotherhood. For a moment I felt comfort; this person was obviously a Christian. Somehow from the far past he knew me.

"I knew it. You're a follower of Satan. Right?"

"What? No! No!" I tried to yell over the thump-thump of the club.

He laughed at me, turned, and left.

I stood frozen. What just happened? Something supernatural had occurred, though I didn't know what, or why. What did that man see in me that led him to believe that I followed Satan? Since college, a broad array of drugs had been part of my life. If it was 2 a.m. and we needed some more coke, we went after it. It didn't matter that we had to call shady characters across town to get it. Most of us did drugs—it was our social enhancer.

But on that night in a Boston club, hopped up on mushrooms and beer, I received a frightful reminder of something that had peeked around at me over the years. The "social additives" that I loved to use and abuse were a gateway into another world, a world that I knew little about—a world that none of us control. Perhaps now it was time to put the college lifestyle away for good. I wanted success in my job, yet I still wanted a good time. I had eased off most of the drugs near the end of my college career, but now I felt it was time to abandon them completely or something bad would happen.

So, I tried to shelve them. I had to function professionally, and frankly, I was freaked out by the connection between drugs and Satan. It was made clear to me that night in the club. Not only was I growing conscious of the spiritual pressure of guilt that confirmed there was going to be a time to pay up, I was getting pressure from the other side. As if dealing with God wasn't enough. Now a dark side was making its presence known to me. And I didn't like it.

░░ ░░ ░░ ░░ ░░ ░░ ░░ ░░ ░░ ░░ ░░ ░░ ░░

I had a similar encounter once along the Long Tom River at the Oregon Country Fair. The counterculture carnival has been held annually the second week of July since 1969 in Veneta, outside of Eugene. The Country Fair emerged out of the Merry Prankster days of Ken Kesey. Ken Kesey, who wrote *One Flew over the Cuckoo's Nest*, was one of the merry pranksters who used to follow the Grateful Dead in their "magic bus."

Back in the day, Kesey was a Beta—my fraternity—at U of O. Each fall he would host an epic party on a smaller scale just for the brothers on his farm outside of Eugene. The magic bus, "Further," featured in Tom Wolfe's *The Electric Kool-Aid Acid Test*, served as the epicenter for the festivities. Partygoers were free to run around the farm all night. Back then, the Country Fair was a place where people could plumb the depths of their inner being by pushing the edges of reality, albeit through hallucinogenic drugs. Today, I hear tell, the Fair is little more than a Burning Man-meets-Starbucks type of gathering. As self-described in their all-things-Fair newsletter, the *Peach Pit*, "The Country Fair is fertile ground in which to incubate an exploration of this cultural shift, of what it means to cultivate a life of the imagination, to be

cultural creatives, Merry Pranksters, holy fools in all we do."
So, you get the picture.

My last visit to the fair was with some frat brothers. That
day I had a run-in similar to the one I had later with the guy
in the Boston club. Throughout the day I saw a man who
wore all black—black Dickie pants, black magician shirt.
Everyone else was dressed for summer. He was dressed for
the Apocalypse.

I kept seeing him everywhere I went. At first I just felt
insecure that he was always standing directly across from
me and staring directly at me, though his silver aviators
blocked my ability to be sure. He wasn't the strangest sight
at the fair, so I chalked it up to paranoia for a good long time,
but finally, standing around a drum circle I looked across
and knew he was looking directly at me.

"Loosen up," he said from across the circle.

I then noticed the horns he had grafted into his head. I
didn't know exactly what that meant; I only knew it made
me uneasy. I knew that the point of being at the carnival, to
some extent, was to be weird. But for me, on that day, something happened upon seeing the horns in that guy's head,
and it crossed the line in my spirit. I was haunted.

I ran from the drum circle all the way to the parking lot

to wait out the day. I was not ready to bare my chest to the demons and put up a fight. I wanted no part of it.

I could feel my spirit becoming more conscious of spiritual things. God hounding you is one thing. Satan in the mix is a whole different game.

## My Grown-up Junior-High Self

You could never string together all the nights we went out during my four years in Boston. They blur in my mind. I do remember one particular night, though. It encapsulates my maturity level as a post-college professional, which isn't saying much. The night began at iconic Fenway Park. A buddy, Adam, was visiting from out of town, so my roommate, Reese, and I took him to a Red Sox game. It wasn't about baseball, though. It was about cutting up. We chucked peanuts at the players warming up in the batter's box and did our best to be obnoxious. We wore out our welcome in a hurry; security finally asked us to leave when fellow spectators got concerned that I was sleeping so deeply. Yes, I had been drinking.

Then we hit the neighboring pool hall. Adam and I ended up sparring with the pool cues, waving them violently across the pool table. As soon as the attendants noticed what we were doing, they rushed down and escorted all three of us out.

Our normal routine for a night out included some time at the Bell In Hand pub for a couple beers and snacks. Bell In Hand was our hangout—all our friends went there. It represented Boston normalcy for me and was conveniently located three blocks from home. But on that particular night we deviated from the norm and went to a more raucous establishment. Walking into Beacon Hill Pub makes you feel like Luke Skywalker walking into that bar in *Star Wars*. We'd go to this alien-type bar periodically when we wanted to turn things up a notch yet not stand out. It was a rougher place.

But tonight even the BHP could not contain us. We finally got kicked out before closing. So we meandered all over town, climbing on the city sculptures, acting like our best drunk selves.

As we tried to negotiate one of the more elusive sculptures that can best be described as a gigantic fixed mobile with large free-swinging arms meant to be propelled by the wind and not ourselves, a panhandler emerged from the shadows—sitting off to the side. He watched our antics for a while. He shouted at us a few times too, popping off, releasing a litany of profanity. We engaged in the profanity-yelling

THE SECRET LIFE OF A FOOL

match for a few minutes. But then the panhandler lay down as if he was going to sleep.

But we continued to harass him and kicked at him a few times.

Reese looked astonished.

"What are you guys doing? Knock it off."

"C'mon, Reese, kick him!"

"Like this!" I said.

We continued roughing him up while we goaded Reese to jump in the fray.

"C'mon, Reese. Just do it."

We finally coerced him. To get us off his back, he feigned and gave a little toe stub but immediately turned on us, livid that we coaxed him to kick a helpless man.

"Yeah, Reese! Do it again." We didn't relent.

"Go to hell, you guys!" And he headed for home. We left the bum to harass Reese and heckled him the whole way back.

That night changed my relationship with Reese—he never looked at me the same. Whenever we'd tell the story, Reese always said how much of jerk I was for doing that. But I would never back down from his accusations, even though I knew he was right.

I wish things had ended differently between Reese and

me. We never reconciled about that night and eventually lost contact.

When I think of that night and so many others, to my shame, I realize how much the apostle Paul and I have in common. He said that he was the chief of sinners. Yeah, Paul, me too.

\* \* \* \* \* \* \* \* \* \* \* \*

Recently I spoke on a Sunday morning in Boise. I woke up to find the Idaho sunshine gleaming across the countryside. The song of the birds filtered through the light and breezy air. The sun blazed through the blue sky and the tree limbs occasionally smacked in the random passing gusts. I had been praying all night that God would peel open souls and bring them to a saving knowledge of Himself. I continued to pray as I walked across the retreat campus, but then I paused: *This is truly life*, I thought. *I can feel so much joy.* Everything good in life was before me: the birds, the gusting breeze, the sun, the blue sky, and the breath of God.

My thoughts that Idaho morning reached all the way back to my house at the U of O, to those evenings when after a long night I'd find myself sitting alone with some cocaine I had reserved for myself. I had found the hollow core of this world—a sense of disgust eased into my blood along with the narcotic. That same song of the birds that brought me such joy now, in that moment had the opposite effect. The rising of the sun should evoke all the best of life, yet I wanted to sink away into oblivion. In that moment, the rising of the sun blocks the idea that there is a chance of sustaining the feeling with more of the same.

It was a hideous place to be and I was, indeed, far from love. I hated it.

I realized that there was a chasm and instead of considering how it might be dealt with, I decided to throw myself into it—to dive all the way inside it, splash around in the murky bottom. It was my relational pit—where I ended up after going my own way.

## My Distant Anchors

I wondered how hard it was for my parents to watch me spin out of control. Did they ever lose hope? If they did, I never knew it. They were wonderful like that.

My dad visited me in Boston on several occasions. He

always did what he could to connect with me, even if it made him a bit uncomfortable. His love was patient but firm. He always spoke truth into my life.

Dad never really knew his father. His dad died when he was ten years old. But before he died Grandpa Palau's testimony was strong in my dad's life. He told Dad that if anything ever happened to him, the Scriptures would parent him. Dad took that to heart. From an early age, he weaned himself on a healthy diet of Psalms and Proverbs. This produced an engaging gentleness in him, such a deep well of love and compassion. I could only look on and admire. But I was always so far from it.

Before Dad became an evangelist, he worked as a banker. He used to press things upon us like tithing, the power of compound interest, and other critical financial principles that he thought we should know. My brothers and I can sit and laugh for hours at how Dad was with us. We can laugh now because at the time it seemed like it was only common parenting pressure. But now, we see what heart it took to keep that pressure going; how all the wisdom he has poured into our lives continues to affect and shape us still.

With Dad, what you see is what you get. And in his case, that's a good thing. You know you're always getting *Luis*, not some trumped-up version of what a dad or evangelist should be. I remember one day as we walked along in Boston we saw, tucked between modern buildings on the way toward Downtown Crossing from the North End, a graveyard and tombstones. We recognized some of the names from history and considered the epitaphs. He mused, and it struck me as so simple then, that he hoped one day we boys would be able to put on his marker, "He wasn't perfect, but he sure loved Jesus." That was Dad: so simple, yet so poignant.

Mom was a beam of light in my life. She was the one forming deeper relationships in the neighborhood—always reaching out to people. Mom treated everyone as if they were the last person on the planet. My parents were missionaries so early on in life that our family didn't own much: no cars, no house, no furniture or anything. But Mom would always work to make our home the hub of activity.

They were very balanced parents and they knew that if anything good was going to happen in our lives it would be God's work. Both were great at trying to get us to read the Bible as they had experienced firsthand the power of the wisdom therein. We weren't very obliging as kids. Dad would go so far as to take us into the garage for family devotions in order to keep it from becoming rote. "If you can't stay awake at the kitchen table," he'd say, "then we'll have devotions in the garage." Along with Bible reading, Mom and Dad pressed the value of literary reading into us. Though I was the most distracted one growing up, this discipline remains in each one of us.

They were also intentional in their efforts to keep the family together and to keep us in touch with each other. To this day everyone—grandkids and all—continues to gather and enjoy our family vacations in central Oregon. The international travel that came along with Dad's occupation as an evangelist was one of the great blessings of our lives. I'm sure some people may doubt that statement, but the truth of the matter is that to the degree that we could ever afford it, Dad tried to intertwine travel as a family with his missions. I gained so much from those trips with the family. Now I have the opportunity to do the same with my three children. What a blessing!

When I moved to Boston, they remained intentional about staying in my life. They'd say they wanted to see the autumn foliage or something like that. So I'd dig around, find a New England bed-and-breakfast, and together we'd discover interesting history about Boston and the surrounding area. We loved that.

They loved my friends and were always gracious and accepting of them. My friends loved them back. They loved Mom for her straight call-it-like-you-see-it perspective and they loved the type of character Dad was: the Argentine preacher man. They respected him. Inside, I loved seeing that play out. I loved that about Dad.

Despite how clearly I try to describe the generosity and transparency of my parents, whenever I share my story, people come to me and say things like, "I know your parents ignored you in all their busyness, so it's no wonder that . . ." or, "It's really hard to try to stand in the shadow of such a great leader, so it's no surprise that . . ." or, "It's not easy being a preacher's kid and having religion shoved down your throat; it's no wonder that . . ."

But there was never anything polarizing about Mom or Dad, nothing that would incite me to go a different direction. I went out of my way to find an alternative life path. If I'm honest, my dad was a cool cat, solid and well respected. People loved him. Maybe that's what I wanted for my life as well. I just took a strange path in my attempt to achieve that. And by the time I realized that I would never garner that type of respect from people where I stood, it was too late. When I thought I had achieved it, it turned out to be a facade.

So, that was Mom. That was Dad. They never conceded our relationship. They always pursued me. I could *see* their love for me, though I was adept at keeping that love at arm's length.

# SIX

# RUN ON FOR A LONG TIME

Above all the grace and the gifts that Christ gives to his beloved is that of overcoming self.

—Francis of Assisi

IT WAS FEBRUARY 1993. I was still living in Boston. It was freezing cold. Dad called me and said, "We're having this crusade and I thought you might want to take some vacation time and join us." That was not really my idea of vacation, so I told him, "No, but thanks anyway, Dad."

"Well, that's okay," he replied. "We just thought you might be interested because this one's in Kingston, Jamaica."

And then, a little light bulb went off in my head. *Ah. I tell him no, and then he springs the information on me that it is* in Jamaica. *Nice, Dad. I get what you're trying to do—I hear what you're saying.*

"Oh. Well, let me think about it."

And I did think about it, right then and there. *Jamaica, huh? Red Stripe beer, on the beach. Yeah, maybe I could move a few things around. Plus, I love to fish.* Then I thought, if Dad was going to work me over, I would return the favor.

"Well . . . okay, Dad. I'll come. But only if you can set me up with a marlin fishing trip." Knowing that he had the connections to make this happen, I pressed him for a little fun for me.

He said he would look around and check on some things. *Cha-ching!*

The next day he called and told me that things were worked out. A new friend, who was helping organize the crusade, had a son who was a tournament marlin fisherman. Dad told me this guy would take me out. Naturally, I told Dad I would come.

So, I was on the hook for the trip.

The invitation was my dad's way of trying to get my attention. He wanted me to be around people who would be a positive influence on me, people who could help me understand what it really meant to follow God.

## New Friends

Upon landing in Kingston, I was met by Robert and Judy Levy and their family. I was immediately impressed with them—with their generosity and honest care for their friends and family. Their lives seemed to revolve around their love for God and others, and I became another person who was on the receiving end of their incredible love and hospitality.

Mr. Levy was a successful businessman who had national impact, but exuded a special tenderness I rarely saw in men. His son, Chris, was the one taking me fishing—an exuberant fellow with obvious passion for fishing, his family, and God.

But most interesting to me was the Levys' daughter, Wendy. At first glance, I thought she was sixteen years old. I had to tell myself to settle down, that I came to fish and to fulfill my obligation to my dad and attend his crusade, not to embarrass myself chasing after a girl. After all, I had to keep up my end of the bargain since he scored me the marlin fishing trip. But I couldn't stop thinking about Wendy after I met her. *Don't get into trouble with these thoughts*, I kept saying to myself. *She's way too young anyhow.*

When I discovered she was my age, lights and sirens were going off. *Calm down, Andrew!* I couldn't help myself. She was sharp and exotic, perfectly blending understandability

in accent and culture—having studied at American board-
ing schools and university—with the sweet Jamaican patois.
It was an unfamiliar sort of beauty to me, one found in the
confidence of a young woman who is captured freshly and
fully by God. I saw that and was drawn to her. She was full of
gratitude and deference to the old things that bind—committed to the good things of life, to fun, and to living life to the
fullest. She was generous and giving. I loved how she cared
for her family. I found it especially interesting how committed she was to a group of young campers she'd served as
counselor to that summer. She met with them regularly, as
a group and one-on-one, intent on building godly character
into their lives. She was fulfilled in God—giving and serving
rather than needy.

But I respected my parents and her parents too much
to go after her. So, I shelved any emotion and intentions, at
least for a while.

The next morning I went fishing with Chris Levy and his
cousin, Andrew. We had a great time on the boat. The day
was beautiful and the water sparkled. What a day! We found
a weed line—a seaweed line that attracts fish—and followed
it for hours, scanning for signs of life. We had a couple of
small strikes, probably wahoo or dolphin, but no hookups.

Then we got a big hit on the line. It was indeed a marlin! The small size of the boat made it a bit awkward to navigate with the marlin on the line, but Andrew managed well enough. I was no help at all while Chris worked his tail off to keep tension on the line. It was one of my first big-game fish experiences and I'll never forget the anticipation of seeing that beautiful fish come out of the water so close to the back of the boat and skip away.

Over the course of our little outing I was able to get to know Chris a bit better. After the battle with the marlin we talked and told stories. I could sense something was different. Chris didn't talk about their antics or crazy parties. Their conversation was tempered with something—something I couldn't put my finger on. Chris began to explain to his cousin that something had radically changed in his life. But why? What prompted the change?

Chris had been a hard-charging partier. He was tough and intense but always had a twinkle of hijinks in his eye. I like that in a person. My respect for these two guys grew while we fished.

As our conversation flourished, I began to see that life change was possible because here was someone who had experienced it. Living proof. I began to ask questions in my head: *What was this all about? Was this possible for me? Could I make this kind of adjustment?* The idea of change was compelling. And if I was honest with myself, I really wanted it. How could I not?

Throughout the week I was able to meet more of Chris and Wendy's friends; many had also recently come alive in their spiritual lives. They talked about how their lives had been turned upside-down: relationships healed, addictions satiated. And they talked about Jesus like He was really alive, like He was actually there among them—as if He were their friend or something. It was strangely beautiful and alluring.

As I thought about their claims, about what had so radically changed them, I thought, *Of course. This is how life should be.* If all the stars were aligned, of course, I would be able to speak with Jesus and walk with Him and offer my whole life to Him. Isn't that what Christianity was? Total surrender to God and immersion in Him?

But the more I thought about it, the more it scared me. The supernatural nature of it all was frightening to me. But in the same way I could sense darkness while at the club in Boston, here I could sense a light and goodness—just as terrifying, and at the same time freeing. It was quite maddening for me to consider. But I did. And the more I hung out with Wendy and her brothers and their friends, the more their lives spoke to me—screamed to me that something *better* was out there.

## Getting Deeper

After our boat trip I continued to hang out with my new-found friends. I sat in on their Bible studies. We did several things together, and surprisingly, I enjoyed all of it. They shared a joy, and it was obvious they shared a common experience as well. Their lives shone to me like the early Jamaican sun beaming off the water. It was almost as if their little community was like a honeycomb, sweet and inter-woven, intricately assembled from the heavens. That might be a bit much, but they were a bit much for this Oregonian-Bostonian transplant who was feeling the spiritual heat. They had been transformed. And radically so. I thought that if this person, Jesus, had done all this for me as well, and wrote these beautiful words of Scripture to me, I would be a fool not to step into this kind of faith. I didn't know what it all meant. But I knew it was powerful.

Perhaps most stark to me was that their faith had not turned them into uninvolved, disassociated people, which is how I often viewed Christians. These people had fun. They were hospitable. They were making an impact on business and civic affairs in their community. They enjoyed each other and outsiders. They loved the outdoors and reveled in its beauty. I remembered the words of my parents when I was growing up. They would often say that Jesus offers life. But not just any life—abundant life. Those words began making sense to me.

While I was seeing the testimony of the Levys and their friends, I was also hearing Dad speak each evening in the Kingston National Stadium. The words of God, through my dad, pounded my heart. Over and over and over. It was as if I was hearing a close friend repeatedly knocking on my front door, yet I refused to open the door. I was standing in the hallway of my heart looking at the door, seeing my old friend there, yet I was unable or unwilling to open the door.

But the constant *knock, knock, knock* on my heart finally made its way through to the inner chamber of my soul.

On the final night, I resolved to really listen to what Dad was saying—to what God wanted to say through him, to me. I not only wanted to listen, I wanted to hear. I wanted to hear God's voice. Maybe now it would come to me in a real way. Maybe now all the faith stuff I encountered as a boy and teenager and even as a rebellious college student—maybe now it would all come together and make sense. I wanted it to.

On that last night of the crusade, I thought maybe a hidden message would emerge and unlock my spiritual door. I expected something different and crazy to happen. While nothing seemed to be happening outwardly, inwardly my desire for this thing was exploding. By the time Dad finished speaking and gave the invitation for those seeking salvation to make their way forward, I determined in my heart that I wanted it. I wanted to be saved. My burden was too heavy, I needed forgiveness, I desired this power to change and to grow, and I wanted peace related to eternity.

I wanted what God was offering.

In that moment, I committed to ending my drug and alcohol use once and for all. I would break off the inappropriate relationships. I told God that I would start going to church. *Yes, God. You heard me correctly. I'll even go to church.* I don't imagine God gets flabbergasted all that often. But I had to think at that moment He was grinning a bit in disbelief at me. I wouldn't blame Him if He did.

When I made these commitments, I felt a sense of relief on the inside. I was excited that I took, what was to me, a bold step of faith. I did not, however, walk forward like so many other people did. Some went in tears, sobbing. *Wow, something must be really wrong with those people,* I thought. Others had a sense of great pride and enthusiasm, rushing to the front. I felt compelled to go, but I did not. Even so, I was proud of my spiritual first step. I had confessed my willingness to begin the stripping-away process of all the junk in my life. I just assumed mine was perhaps a less emotional approach. It was a good night.

I wanted to tell someone. My mind immediately went to Wendy. I was excited and it occurred to me that now there would be a better connection with her. I couldn't wait to tell her, "Hey, this thing that you guys found? So did I!" I also felt like I should tell my parents. But then doubt settled in. *I better just ease into it and not freak them out. What if I tell them but fall back into my old way of life and let them down?* It's not about proving or letting down. It's about the relationship with Jesus. But at that point, I still had not grasped that truth. So I told myself I'd wait to tell my parents, but I would tell Wendy.

After the service, there was a party for all the staff and volunteers. I attended it with Wendy. Even as we walked together at the party, I sensed this new relationship between us growing. We enjoyed each other's company. We walked by the pool together and, somewhat awkwardly I'm sure, I finally blurted out that I prayed the prayer during Dad's final session.

"I really think this is my new direction," I told her.

"I can't believe it. I'm thrilled for you, and have been praying for this, Andrew."

She affirmed me in the experience and we both gushed about it. But the next words out of her mouth were, "You have to tell your parents, Andrew." My heart shuddered a bit, but I knew she was right.

If you hear Dad tell the story of how I shared the news, he would say that I ran into their hotel room, jumped up on their bed, and yelled, "I did it! I did it! I've become a Christian." That's how he received the news, but I remember it differently. I remember an awkward encounter—for me anyway —filled with fear and uncertainty.

Nonetheless, my parents encouraged me and affirmed my decision. They had seen faith conversions like mine thousands of times throughout their lives—people making decisions at the crusades. They knew what to expect. They didn't want to discourage me in any way, though later they did tell me that they sensed hesitation in my profession of faith. They held a "Let's see what happens" posture. But they still trusted that God had begun a work in my life and were confident that, as He's always done, He would complete it.

## The Way Home

After that final crusade service on Sunday, February 14, everyone left the next day—Mom and Dad back to Oregon and me back to Boston. Wendy took me to a craft market on our way to the airport. That morning I began to feel myself changing, even if only in small ways. Not only spiritually, but my interaction with Wendy continued to bloom as well.

My rule of not getting involved with my parents' friends' daughters was fizzling. But this relationship was so unlike all my previous relationships with women. I viewed Wendy in a strange and wonderful new light. I esteemed her in a way foreign to me. And it wasn't simply because of her beauty—though she is the most beautiful girl in the world—it was because she was insightful and peaceful and I found myself wanting to know what she thought about everything. This was new territory for me. What was growing between Wendy and me was altogether different.

The fact that I was simultaneously experiencing a spiritual awakening made it even more special. The dark waters were changing in my life, and my relationship with Wendy was part of the stirring gleam.

After we dillydallied at some gift shops and said our good-byes, I embraced her, gave her a kiss on the cheek, and boarded the plane back to Boston.

After the crusade, Dad called me almost daily with tips and encouragement and advice on how to cultivate my new relationship with Jesus Christ. The greatest thing about Dad's counsel is that he was not overbearing. Though he cared and offered advice, he gave me freedom and space to learn on my own. Many of the things he suggested to me, I did: things as simple as daily Bible reading, developing a consistent prayer life, and even going to church. My responsiveness came as a total surprise to me.

When I stepped back into the swing of things in my Boston life, I knew I needed to address several bad relationships—some to break off completely, some to apologize for my hurtful behavior.

I went to church. I told my close buddies, Tom and Vic, about my decision, as well as my boss and my roommate. My roommate was an illegal Scottish immigrant who had once entertained the idea of marrying one of his lesbian friends in order to attain citizenship. He was a little off, a bit nuts.

We were a perfect pair. When I told him about my conversion, his reply was classic: "Rubbish!"

## My Rubbish Faith

So I tried this new faith. I tried my utmost to follow through with the commitments I made with regard to the way I lived. Weeks went by, but it only took one evening for it all to come crashing down. I failed miserably in a moment and got "pie-faced," as we called it, at some random bar.

The remorse of that night sent me into a tailspin. I was so embarrassed. How would I tell my dad what I had done? I was ashamed I had made this very public change and then failed so very publicly. *How could I be so sincere and yet fail so miserably? What happened?*

I thought I did everything the way I was supposed to. It didn't take long for the shame and embarrassment to send me spiraling out of control once more. My old way of life roared back with a vengeance. It was like a tidal wave—pummeling me into the ocean floor and then dragging me out to sea. I felt anchorless.

As I reflected on the Jamaica trip, I knew I felt different. But was I changed? Though I had sought to end the drug and alcohol use and the relationships, my old self still persisted. Maybe a better way to say it is I still wanted what I knew I could get. But there was also this moral side to me, the side of me that wanted to do good—to be good. Maybe I felt this way because I knew who I was, or who I'd been. And though I still desired the feelings that came with dissipation, I also wanted to feel that I was on the right path in life.

So, a war had begun in my heart. On the one hand, I wanted to reach out and touch a God who delighted in people who were trying to be good. Perhaps that's what I thought this confession of faith was: a wink from God letting me know I was okay and on the right track. But on the other hand, I wanted to party on the weekends. I think I wanted the security of religion but was unwilling to commit to anything that would jeopardize my "good time."

In the Bible story about the rich young ruler, the young man obviously has life by the tail. He's powerful and wealthy. But even more than that, he desires to follow the new, popular rabbi in town, Jesus of Nazareth. He approaches Jesus and asks what he must do to enter the kingdom of God. Jesus tells him, "You shall not commit adultery, you shall not murder, you shall not steal, you shall not give false testimony, honor your father and mother."

The rich young ruler is ecstatic.

"I have kept all these commandments," he says. As I read this passage in the Bible, I can almost feel this young guy's pride swelling off the page.

*This is great,* I imagine him thinking. *I have money and power, and now all I need to do is keep these commandments, which I already do. I'm in!*

But Jesus is not finished with His kingdom list.

"Good," says the rabbi. "You already keep these commandments—that's fantastic. Now there's one more thing I need you to do."

Here is where Jesus exposes the heart of the rich young ruler.

"You still lack one thing. Sell everything you have and give to the poor, and you will have treasure in heaven. Then come, follow Me."

This saddened the rich young ruler for obvious reasons. He was rich! He derived his identity from what he possessed and what he could control, keeping the commandments. I suppose he was so attached to his current way of life that he found his identity in his wealth and power.

I related to the rich young ruler. Not because I possessed loads of cash or wielded power over others. Rather, I had built my own kingdom, so to speak. And in that kingdom I was king. My wealth was all my friends who loved the wild and crazy Andrew. My power was the enormous ego I derived from all my shenanigans. I mean, I could fill in the blanks in my own little economy on the whole wealth and power scenario. No matter how you sliced it, I was the rich young ruler.

Seems ironic using this story to describe myself, since the last time my dad spoke at the Jamaican crusade, the night I made my decision, he spoke about the rich young ruler. There I was at the crusade listening to my dad preach while I was having an inner dialogue with Jesus, asking Him what I needed to do to get into His kingdom. I thought the recitation of a prayer would suffice. But a rote prayer without the sincerity that comes with real brokenness is hollow if it is not done with a sincere heart and an honest commitment to change—in my case, seriously committing myself to Jesus Christ as Lord and Savior. My prayer to God sounded like, "Sure, God, You know I want these things. Relief from this guilt, power to show some self-control, confidence about my future and about eternity. I'll do good and follow Your commands." The core of my prayer, however, was empty because I was not willing to dive into Jesus Christ. I wanted His free gift, but despite all that Dad and so many others had made clear, I wanted it to be cheap. In fact, I was counting on it being cheap.

Years later I came across the writings of Dietrich Bonhoeffer. Bonhoeffer was a German scholar and pastor who taught Christian theology to young German students attending seminary in the 1930s and 1940s. Bonhoeffer's was a radical life. Seeing the growing threat of the Third Reich, he joined a covert group determined to assassinate Adolf Hitler.

Bonhoeffer was captured following the failure of the murder plot and was executed. But during his imprisonment he wrote a wonderful book titled *The Cost of Discipleship*, which questioned a Christian faith devoid of conviction, devoid of commitment, devoid of sacrifice. To Bonhoeffer, Christianity was not a joke. If a person determines to follow Jesus Christ, that person must be willing to follow in Jesus' footsteps. That meant dying. Bonhoeffer led by his actions.

He used the phrase "cheap grace" in the book. The phrase means that the people who are unwilling to count the cost, people who are unwilling to give up their very selves, are not worthy to be called Christians. To Bonhoeffer this was religion without a soul; it cheapened the grace that had cost Jesus His life.

If Bonhoeffer had been standing next to me at the Jamaican crusade, he would have grabbed my shoulder and said, "Now listen here, Andrew. Do you know what you're doing here? Do you know what you're getting yourself into? This is not only fire insurance! This is you telling Jesus Christ, the living Son of God, that you realize what His death means to your life. It means that His gift to you should evoke passion to be in a real relationship with Him. You're not deciding on what religion to be affiliated with. You're telling God, through His Son, that you recognize what a rebel you really are. You're calling out to God to lift you from the miry pit—the junk in your life that you think is great, but is ripping your soul to shreds. And to replace it all with His Son. Andrew, you're beginning a life; you're joining a heavenly family. Do you understand that?"

But I didn't understand that. I had the rich young ruler complex. I wanted God without giving myself up.

# SEVEN
# THE GLIMMERING GIFT

Now is our chance to choose the right side. God is holding back to give us that chance. It won't last forever. We must take it or leave it.

—C. S. Lewis

I THANK GOD for guilt. Most of us hate guilt. But guilt played a vital role in my life. That role was made evident when I accepted an invitation from Wendy to come back to the island so we could reconnect after my recent "conversion."

Wendy and I had remained in contact after my first visit. In fact, she was supposed to come to Boston to see me. One day she called to discuss an opportunity she had to come for a visit.

"Hey, Andrew, I have a friend in Boston who wants me to come visit. Do you think that would be okay with you? I mean, really, how would that be?"

"Oh, that would be great." We talked about her coming up and us hanging out, and I heard myself repeating to her that everything was fine. But she didn't know that I had already returned to my former way of life. She had no clue the extent my failure had reached. She knew that I had made a decision to follow God that night two months prior, but that's it.

I thought I wanted religion in my life, but I couldn't shake the old me that seemed too strong for any religious experience. Was it just a fluke? Had I been right about religion all this time—that it was nothing but a crutch for the weak, fine for some but not for me? A part of me wished that was not true—knew it was not true; the other part of me was looking for the party.

But then Wendy blindsided me. I was all fired up for her coming and then she changed her tune. She called again for what I thought would be a conversation to work out her travel details. I didn't expect what I heard from her.

"I can't come up there, Andrew. It's not the right thing for us right now. You know?" She was dead on. All I could do was agree. I felt relieved, though I desperately wanted to see her again. That's when she sprung the Jamaica return trip on me.

"But, Andrew," she said, "you are welcome back here any time. If you get the chance to come back, you could go fishing and stay with the family again—they would love that, and I would love to see you. It would be great."

Her quasi-offer, however, presented a quandary for me. I was about to be transferred back to Oregon from Boston. An opportunity arose and I took it. I had no idea any of this would transpire. After I made the transfer, it would be hard for me to scrape up the funds to go all the way to Jamaica. I wouldn't have a window to do much of anything except work. If I didn't go in the next week or two, I knew I would not go anytime soon, if ever. I had to make a decision.

My mind was flooded with thoughts about my spiritual despair, my transfer, and Wendy's proposal. But though my uneasiness about my spiritual condition pervaded, I was confident I could go back to Jamaica and visit Wendy and her family, playing off my spiritual fallout. After all, I was a pro at playing things off. How could I go wrong: me in the Caribbean, with a beautiful Jamaican woman, with nothing to do but fish and walk the beach? Seemed perfect. She'd never know the difference.

Then my spirit stirred within me. Was there ever an end to my double-mindedness? How could I think so defiantly about my return to Jamaica? The Levys would see through me anyway. What was I thinking? I felt like the man James wrote about in the Bible who forgets what he looks like right after he sees himself in the mirror.

*This is me.*

*Okay. What did I look like?*

*Who am I again?*

I didn't want to be that guy. I wanted to know who I was— or more accurately who I could be. Who could I be to Wendy? Who could I be to my parents?

*God, who am I?*

## My Return

Just like she had driven me to the airport on the first trip, Wendy picked me up on this second trip. I was blown away that she was into me and, of course, I was into her. How would this all pan out? On the first trip I was thinking Red Stripe beer and *I know how to handle this Christian thing.* Now I was flying back thinking, *What am I doing? This Christian thing is overwhelming me!* Normally I would have been taking the path of least resistance, but in this instance I was going against who I was.

The only explanation I had was that my initial conversion was still seeping into me. God was still hounding me. Still, I had to tell Wendy and her family, "Yeah, guys . . . I tried to do the faith thing, but failed. I'm back to my old ways."

What was I thinking! I couldn't tell them that.

When she arrived at the airport she said, "Let's get some dinner. Then we'll go home and see the family."

So we drove to dinner. But the place was significantly more romantic than she intended the evening to be. Ivor's Restaurant was an old plantation house that clung to the side of the mountain looming over Kingston—the city shimmered in the heat. The candles were lit, and the staff focused only on us because no one was in the restaurant. It was picturesque. After a bit of catching up and small talk, Wendy asked me a direct question: "Andrew, why did you really come out here?" I normally avoided such direct conversation and would typically have been quite tipsy in this scenario. So, I fumbled for words.

"I came to see you and the family, of course. I'm excited to hang out with Chris and go fishing." I blabbed and stumbled. I'm sure I did not convince her. Then Wendy looked at me straight in the eyes and told me, "Andrew, I need you to know that whatever your intentions, Jesus Christ is the most important thing in my life. I'm glad you've come. But I won't let anything interfere with that most important relationship."

I could have shown indignation or displeasure in her words. But amazingly they soaked right into me with ease.

"Of course," I replied. "I wouldn't . . . blah, blah, blah." I have no idea how I responded, but I'm sure it was completely ridiculous. Truth be told, I was happy to be with her at that moment—happy to be with her family and in that wonderful place. I let the moment linger. We ate our dinner to the song of our banter. I had no problem being second.

The rest of my first week in Jamaica was very much a holiday. It coincided with Wendy's family taking a few days' break together at the home of a friend—a little house on the north coast, a classic older-style cottage. That's where we all hung out. The doors would open wide toward the sea in the morning, and we enjoyed the beach day after day.

One of Chris's friends, Steve Smith, and his family also went along with us to the north coast. He was an influencer in the whole group of people that Wendy and Chris hung out with—very instrumental in communicating how things had changed so dramatically with all these people, including himself and his wife.

During that great holiday week, Wendy and I progressed further in our relationship. Even in those short first days we began showing more affection for one another, going deeper in our conversations and just having fun. It was all I could do not to give her a real kiss by week's end. But I had to kiss her, right? She even asked me, "Andrew, why haven't you kissed me?" To which I replied, "It's because I respect you, Wendy. I need to be careful with you—I am going to be careful with you."

And I meant what I said; I was sincere.

But it only made Wendy want to kiss me more. Go figure.

Knowing the place I had come from and what I was doing with Wendy, I not only told her this; I told myself this. I had to be careful. And I was.

## Confronted with Transformation

As the week progressed and as we all enjoyed beach time and playing cards, concerns about my spiritual condition began to creep into my mind. I had some unfinished business I needed to take care of. I knew that. Just, when?

At the end of one of our late-night Kaluki sessions, as people trailed off and headed to bed and Wendy and I contemplated how to make our inconspicuous move to go sit under the stars, I got into a discussion with Chris and Steve. They began to question me, rightly, wondering about my spiritual life.

"Andrew, how's it going?" asked Steve. "You made that decision weeks ago; what's going on with it?"

I told them flat out that I was struggling. I made the decision and wanted to live better, but I was really struggling. I wondered if it was going to work for me, despite my good intentions. I was relieved by their sympathetic responses—it meant a lot that they would even care to ask. They told me not to freak out and reassured me that we all needed one another. That spoke volumes to me. I had heard stories about Chris. I knew he really pinned it, even more than I did from the sound of things. So to know what he had been through and the radical change he had made, to hear him affirming me and encouraging me . . . it was the world to me. Finally, someone related to me, someone who knew similar struggles. They knew my struggle and they weren't panicking.

Steve told me, "The one thing I find to be the most important thing to growing in faith and in relationship with God is to meet with Him regularly and hear Him, letting Him speak to me. His Word, the Bible, is how He speaks. And if we take the time to spend with Him, then we find Him . . . So what I do is that I discipline myself to get up early each day and ask God to speak directly to me through His Word—away from the noise and the clutter that presses in on us all. I'm doing it tomorrow first thing and before breakfast. Do you want to join me?"

I said yes. And so we met.

We sat in the living room in the early morning and opened the doors wide. He had been reading in Romans and suggested we just keep going where he'd last left off. I told him that would be great. So that's what we did. He told me it was his habit to get on his knees when he read and prayed in the mornings. So I followed suit. And we read Romans 12.

I can remember it like it was yesterday. I can hear Steve's voice reading the words.

Therefore, I urge you, brothers and sisters, in view of God's mercy, to offer your bodies as a living sacrifice, holy and pleasing to God—this is your true and proper worship. Do not conform to the pattern of this world, but be transformed by the renewing of your mind. Then you will be able to test and approve what God's will is—his good, pleasing and perfect will. For by the grace given me I say to every one of you: Do not think of yourself more highly than you ought, but rather think of yourself with sober judgment, in accordance with the faith God has distributed to each of you.[8]

As we read this passage, I was caught off guard. I had no idea what was going on. I didn't know what it meant. I began to cry. And I couldn't recall any time in my life when I cried like that. I was an English major. I knew how to understand things; I knew how to read into texts. But I had no idea what I was hearing. The meaning of the passage eluded me. Something deep was there before me. It felt like life or death, but it was obscure and I began to sob. Crazy!

"Andrew, it's okay," Steve said. "This is what you need to do. You need to come with us to the mountains, to Greenwich. We've done it for the last three years, just a little Bible study and gathering together. We go to hear from God."

I wanted to go. But I would have to change my ticket home. My mind raced through the details, the things I needed to do to extend my trip. Then the wheels in my brain stopped. I completely overlooked my going-away party. My best friend in the world, Tom, had been planning my going-away party from Boston for weeks. He made sure everyone I knew was going to be there. He and Vic had made such an effort planning the party, and now I was considering not showing up for it. My own party! How could I do this to them?

But I knew I had things to work through, questions that needed answers. What was I supposed to do?

Back and forth my brain bounced—between the scenarios, between what I knew I was being drawn to and loyalty to my friends. It was agonizing to think through.

So I called Tom and told him what I was thinking. I tried to describe to him how deep my embarrassment was while communicating to him what I was going through. He was initially angry. On the other hand, it's how Tom and everyone else had come to know me—all he heard is that I was blowing off my own party to meet up with some girl in Jamaica—classic. It didn't matter the reason I was missing the party; they just chalked it up to me being me. The stories I heard from the party were that they all had a great time and saluted my total lack of respect for others to do what I wanted. I guess that was a fitting way for them to remember me, fitting and sad.

So, I had decided, and I called Steve.

"I'll do it."

**The Blue Mountains**

I found myself the next morning, headed up the stepladder Blue Mountain roads. The switchbacks ascend to a special little house tucked on the side of one of the peaks, amid the coffee fields. Stunning, really.

The plan for the weekend entailed having a good time together, building relationships, and enjoying the beauty of this place. Interspersed throughout were times of prayer and singing, teaching and reading the Bible on certain topics, times of intentional discussions on what we were learning. It was cultivated to be a time where each person could allow God to get to a remote place within. Being surrounded by the magnificent countryside and the coffee fields made it easy to put my mind on God.

Out of the Bible teaching times, I began wrestling with some of the thoughts about the Holy Spirit. This pushed me out of my pre-established understanding of God. The Christian faith is not only about your past or your future—your past issues being dealt with and your eternal standing being dealt with—though it would be worth it if it was only about all of that. For me, it is much more personal, dealing with my today.

The concept that God is with me and close to me—not far off and disconnected, but alive and near—comforted me and rattled me as well. When I began to see God as *there* and real and living and wanting a better way for me, my spirit shook. Not shaking with an unhealthy fear, but in an intimate way. This was a teaching relating to God as a personal, present God.

We also focused on passages that revealed the incredible nature of God. Who was I in relation to who God is? That was my question, and that question was being answered as I slowly began to understand who God is in a personal way but also who He is as a massive, royal King of kings whose purity alone would annihilate my very existence. I began to understand that this holy God could not, because of His nature, be in a relationship with a human whose nature was such as mine was. Someone who was unrepentant, living a life cluttered by sin.

On the final morning before our departure, during our last Bible study and worship time, my inner dialogue went like this. *God, everyone else here has experienced You in this deep way, but why can't I? I want to meet You in a personal way, yet fully acknowledging Your holiness. If You're real, I have to know.* My mind rested on this theme—*Reveal Yourself to me.*

The problem with the nature of my appeal is that there was an assumption in it that God had one more thing to do for me. I wanted all the good things of God. I wanted the monkey of guilt off my back. I wanted to be free of the shame and guilt of my life. I needed power to live my life, and I had never had it. I wanted assurance of eternity in this place called heaven—like the sparkling city I saw in the sky as a young boy.

But God did not have one more thing to do for me. His parting words from the cross were, "It is finished." His work on humankind's behalf, with regard to the salvation that everyone needs, was completed in that moment. Now He waits on our response.

And yet my mind persisted. With everything going on during the retreat, where our spiritual discussions led and how everyone else seemed to be experiencing real interaction with God, I thought it was only natural for me to challenge God to simply reveal Himself to me. I was sincere, but looking back it seems an audacious and even dangerous line of thinking, but I wanted and fully expected God to literally stand before me. I was basically asking God for a miracle, for Him to supernaturally appear to me. But isn't that exactly what we had been talking about all weekend? The longer I sang outwardly and cried out to the Lord inwardly, and the more I watched everyone else experiencing God in such powerful ways, the more I wondered what was keeping me from God.

I thought I had done what I needed to do—all the "Christian stuff"—Bible study, worship through singing, extended times of prayer. But I was missing the point. There was something more. An obstacle impeded my path to God. The obstacle was me.

I wanted all the good things of God. Turns out that God was waiting all along—running toward me, seeking me, searching for me, calling me. And there I was: I had finally stopped running but was waiting for Him to do something. For me it was like an awkward pause between two young kids on a dance floor. You're not sure what you should say or who is going to say it—both think the other person should speak. You're not sure where to put your hands, so you fumble around awkwardly tugging on your suit jacket.

All I could concentrate on was this proof. I wanted God to prove Himself to me. I stood there like the doubting disciple—

Thomas—who wouldn't believe that Jesus Christ had risen from the dead until he could see the nail scars for himself. "Let me put my fingers in the place . . ." That was me. "Show me the scars, Jesus!"

I don't recommend this type of response to God, but there I stood, demanding a response from Him. I said to Him, "Well, You're God and You have all the awesome power of the world before You. Why don't You do this thing for me; so simple, just stand before me? Then I will know and will never forget." I literally thought my encounter with Him would be something like that. As if He would let me poke around in His being to make sure He was who He said He was.

*Oh look, there's God standing before me, just as I asked.*

Then I would know. Then I would be confident that He was real, that this relationship was real, and that He wanted me—He really wanted me.

I spent so much time living as if He didn't exist, as if the only person who mattered was the one looking back at me in the mirror. I secretly wanted the Doubting Thomas encounter. I wanted to poke around in a God who carries life scars just like mine, a God who "gets it" and is big enough to shoulder my doubt and open Himself up to me.

But in that moment up in the Blue Mountains of Jamaica, a spiritual awareness was overtaking me. It wasn't like the familiar high from the drugs I had taken so many times before. It wasn't the horrifying recognition of a dark force pressing on me. It wasn't the spiritual help of guilt hounding me. It was something altogether different. Not a feeling, but an approaching presence.

And then it happened. My heart welled up with a plea. *God, what is keeping me from You?* In that moment, God did what I asked. Differently. God acquiesced to my longing, to my selfish tugging at His suit jacket.

*Do you really want to know what is keeping you and Me apart?*

*Yes, God, of course. What is it?*

Then God opened my eyes and granted my wish.

There before me was all the junk in my life. All those unholy things that were keeping me away from the heavenly relationship I was intended for.

I was horrified.

There before me was all the harshness and the darkness of my lying, cheating, stealing; all the addictions, the abusive relationships, my arrogance and pride . . . it was all there stacked up as high as I could see—a wall of seemingly insurmountable sin.

Overwhelmed, I fell on my face stricken, my body heaving with remorse. I wailed out, "God, how could I have been such a fool?" I begged Him at that moment. "Will You please forgive me? Please take what is before me and send it away? I cannot live with any of it. What hope is there when all of this is in me?"

God's compassionate response was straight out of Scripture. "If you confess your sin, Andrew, I will be faithful and I am able to forgive you of your unrighteousness. I will clean you out. I will take it away as far as the east is from the west. I will remember it no more."

The sobs began to rack my frame. Just like those who had gone forward at the stadium. I had wondered if they didn't realize how awkward it was. Now, I didn't care how I looked. I wasn't even aware that I was face down on the patio. I was caught up in dialogue with God Almighty as He did this deep spiritual work. In a very real way, I was struggling for life. I was hanging by a thread.

I was in new territory. Never had I confessed my dark ways to God or to anyone. And as He revealed to me what I was without Him, I fell deeper into Him. The guilt and shame that stripped me down to the bone was the catalyst with which He breathed new life into me. My shame broke me; it was the evidence that convinced me there was a better way. It allowed me to see myself for who I was—created by God, in need of cleansing, so I could become His child.

God cleaned me out that morning. He ripped the sin from me; issue by issue, act by act, it was showcased before me. I would cry forgiveness for it and He took it, burying it deep never to be seen. He kept revealing and forgiving, over and over. It was as if someone was taking a smooth river stone and scouring my heart and my insides, purifying me. It was painful, but the more it was brought to my attention and forgiven, the more I wanted to plumb the depths of my soul. I would take this chance to say search my soul and take over; inhabit every part of my being. No room was closed.

As this was going on inside of me, all anyone could see was prostrate Andrew on his face weeping. Chris, Steve, and Joe came to me and whispered prayers to me, encouraging me not to shortchange the moment. As I struggled through prayer and heaved with confession and relaxed into forgiveness, they prayed that God would work deeply in my heart; they prayed for the stone scouring to continue and for me to remain open to God's mighty Spirit.

Eventually, we went into the living room where I could be alone as I continued in this inner confrontation. I remained in the room for three hours as I was not just scoured but disinfected by God.

And then it ended.

Exhausted, I got up off of my face and looked down the mountain in front me. My heart was filled with indescribable joy. I could see clearly. The natural world around me appeared new and shone with brilliance. And I was at peace within it. Peace beyond my ability to comprehend.

As I looked around, absorbing the moment, I whispered to God, "I will tell everyone what You've done."

He replied, "Yes, you will." I began to cry once more, but this time out of incredible relief and gratitude that God was willing to do that for me. All I had to do was ask Him to release my burden and He did. He released me.

## Coal on My Lips

I remember Bible stories like most remember fairy tales from their childhood. One story in particular sticks out to me because it was the quintessential "Give your life to God and Christian ministry" type of story. I would hear youth leaders talk about this story; my dad would use it to challenge his listeners to consider a life focused on God's mission.

But to me it carries deep personal value. It is a shocking story that my own conversion mirrors. It remains dear to my heart; it is the closest description I have ever heard to what I experienced for myself that day.

A certain prophet from the Bible named Isaiah encounters God. Isaiah sees God sitting on an ethereal throne canopied with fiery angels—each with six wings. Two of their wings cover their faces, another two their feet, and they fly with the final set. As they hover over God they volley back and forth, "Holy, holy, holy is the Lord God Almighty! His bright glory fills the whole earth!" The foundations tremble at the sound of the angelic voices. What a scene.

Isaiah, upon seeing this, realizes that he is in the presence of the holy God. The angels are chanting it and the earthquake tells him that the end of his time in the presence of God is near.

So the prophet cries out, "Doom! It's Doomsday! I'm as good as dead! Every word I've ever spoken is tainted—blasphemous even! And the people I live with talk the same way, using words that corrupt and desecrate. And here I've looked God in the face! The King! God-of-the-Angel-Armies!" But then one of the angels flies over to the prophet with a flaming piece of coal from the altar and touches his lips with it. The angel says, "Look. This coal has touched your lips. Gone is your guilt, your sins wiped out."

The altar is an image of the cross on which Jesus paid the penalty due for sin. Isaiah's experiences led to immediate and radical change in his life. God had a purpose for

Isaiah and did the work necessary in his life to allow him to accomplish it. So, though the act of wiping away guilt and sin is necessary for spiritual salvation, it is also necessary for the right here and now. That's what Isaiah experienced. And that's what God did with me in the Blue Mountains—that's what God wants to do with each one of us.

The scene with Isaiah ends with a question from God: "Whom shall I send? Who will go for us?"

Isaiah responds, "Here am I, send me."[9] That was my automatic response when I experienced this very personal yet holy God as well: "I'll tell everyone." When we dare enter into relationship with God through the beautiful gateway of guilt and confession, God touches us with His presence for all eternity. For Isaiah, it was the coal to his lips. For me, it was the glimmering gift of guilt searing my soul—the scouring agent of God.

EIGHT
# THE WORLD AS NEW

Behold, I am making all things new.

—Jesus Christ of Nazareth, Son of God
Revelation 21:5 ESV

WHEN I WALKED INTO the orphanage to bring my daughter, Sadie, home she had no idea I was coming. A beautiful baby from Ethiopia, Sadie lay vulnerable and open to the harshness of life. But when I entered the room and picked her up in my arms, she became mine.

This is what God did for me—what He does for each one of us. I had been struggling through life as a spiritual orphan, and then God stepped into my life, picked me up, and said, "You are Mine."

That intense morning in the Blue Mountains out on the veranda was the day I found a new eternal home. I inexplicably found myself on the veranda floor—my orphanage bed— looking around at the world with brand-new eyes. Like Sadie when I picked her up, I lay vulnerable, but only for a moment. Then God picked me up off the veranda floor, held me in His arms, and marveled at me like any father.

On that day I came face-to-face with a God who was different from anything I had ever dreamt of or considered before. For having had the experience, I have no option. Above all else in life, I want other people to know that same feeling. I was made alive and finally recognized that I had so many people who loved me. God showed me that. I was cared for and loved and all I wanted to do was tell people about this thing I had found in Jesus.

I was broken into pieces, but God collected all the pieces and put them back together. In that moment I was remade— pressed into this person who was being formed by love and mercy.

Now, ever since that Blue Mountain morning, my heart burns with the story of what God did in me. It wasn't only my insides that were scrubbed clean, it was the fact that I had found my spiritual Father—and am loved for who I am.

I want to share about being born and finding my place in Jesus. Birth is bloody and there's anguish involved. But what comes of it is wonderful. I can't understand why this isn't talked about more, why some look at newness as something that isn't sophisticated enough to be credible. But innocence can't be held down, for it comes from God. We can't make things new. We can't change darkness to light or reverse aging. Doctors perform surgery, but God is the Healer. We can only mend things with Band-Aids. We need the Creator and the life He brings.

When I picked Sadie up that day, I held her close. I could hear her breaths slowly emanating from her nose. I touched my cheek to hers. I could smell her newness—that baby smell that everyone loves. So precious. So fragile. So wonderful.

Birth is a fragrance. It causes each one of us to marvel at it and desire more of it. You want to be bathed in it, enveloped by it.

Spiritually speaking, then, it is inevitable that this fragrance of new life will overtake you. We love the new baby smell because it is so pure, so innocent. That morning, I became new. I became a child again. I had that pure baby smell and God rubbed His cheek on me.

How does it feel to consider that God would rub His cheek upon yours? Can you feel His breath upon you now?

## The Filament Within

I was scoured after my time of intense prayer; the cleansing newness of life overwhelmed me. Wendy noticed it on our trip back down those stepladder mountain roads. That was reassuring to me. I encountered God in the most real way imaginable—by His grace.

The clarity with which I could see things all around me was undeniable. It was as though someone had turned on the lights of my soul. Christ is the current that ignites the filament within us and fills us with the light of life—vibrant and wonderful, pushing darkness aside. We become vibrant beings living in communion with Him—the very place we were created to be.

One thing about God that amazes me is how He draws us to Himself and as we grow closer to Him, we grow closer to each other. My Blue Mountain time was as refreshing as it was intense. All the people with me there supported me and told me that they would pray for me. We sang together, ate together, and worshipped together, and all these years later, we continue to. My relationship with Wendy began to root deeply within me, as if God had removed the guilt-governor in my heart, allowing me to respond to her in the purest of ways. Perhaps more than any other consequence of my new life, my relationship with Wendy illustrated just how deep Father God loves me.

I sat in the car on the way down the mountains humbled, holding Wendy's hand, knowing I had experienced a new beginning in every way imaginable. I could feel the filament in my spirit glowing, flooding my life with light.

# NINE

# A MOVE TOWARD HOPE

Therefore, since we have been justified through faith,
we have peace with God through our Lord Jesus
Christ, through whom we have gained access by faith into
this grace in which we now stand. And we boast in the hope
of the glory of God. Not only so, but we also glory in our
sufferings, because we know that suffering produces perseverance; perseverance, character; and character, hope.
And hope does not put us to shame, because God's love
has been poured out into our hearts through the Holy Spirit,
who has been given to us.

—The apostle Paul
Romans 5:1-5


IS MY STORY important?

Yes it is, and for the same reason yours is important.

Because it deals with the reality that God is alive in this

world. I tell my story in hopes that it will draw you closer to an understanding of the grace and mercy that God offers. Otherwise, I would most likely just keep it to myself. It's not easy to share all this; I think of the impact that dragging out some of the stories has on my family's emotions, on how my children will view me. If there were not the possibility that this will help someone, sharing these stories with you would be meaningless.

But we all want to move toward hope. We all want to know that there is a way out of the hole we're in.

All those religious and biblical pictures you hear about—"He will make you white as snow," or "The wages of sin is death, but the gift of God is eternal life"—can become cliché to those who have heard them their whole life. Words without action are meaningless. But join the two and you have profound truth—the kind of truth you can see and know, truth that carries power. When you experience rebirth; when you experience the wiping away of your guilt and shame; when you experience redemption, knowing then more clearly than ever that what you were facing was death, words take on a new and vibrant meaning. It's as real as the Jamaican mountains, the mountains where I found God.

## Found and Known

"I knew I needed to go somewhere, anywhere but where I was. Reality was crumbling all around me and I just wanted to be in a safe place."

That's what Derrik told me when I met him at the front of my home church in Portland, Oregon. His connection to my church was completely random—he had come once, years earlier when he was a boy. For some reason it stuck in his mind. And there we stood, talking about how he was being sucked into a black hole of drug use. He told me of this odd desire to run toward God and how, the night before, he was compelled to come back to this place.

The message I shared that morning was exactly what I've shared with you in these pages. I invited people in that moment to ask God to forgive them, to come into their lives, as He had done in mine. I encouraged them to say thank you for these things and for heaven. Not with my words, but by their souls connecting and conversing with the living God. Afterward I invited people to come forward so we could rejoice with them and pray with them.

My emotions always soar after having the opportunity to remember and share the great news of Jesus' redemption, but Derrik's presence there that day was more important than how I felt about it personally. After the music had ended and everyone began to leave, Derrik and I sat and talked about his journey.

He told me his whole story and we sobbed together. His story was so much like my own: the distance between him and God, the lies he began to believe as he opened up his soul to whatever desired to fill it, and the awful grip of drugs on him. I knew what he was experiencing and I knew how that pain had begun to lift, even dissipate in that moment when we prayed and shared.

But even now as I reflect on Derrik's story, I am impressed with "why" questions.

Why God? Why now?

Like me, Derrik arrived at a point in his life where he didn't feel safe in his own thoughts. Left alone, Derrik and I chose the drug path. On that particular path, you *feel* as if you have control, but it's really just smoke and mirrors. The control is the substance. I'll take it a step further and say that the control is spiraling blackness; it is evil.

There are some who will read this and say, "But I'm not struggling with drugs or alcohol or anything like those vices. I can't relate." Great! The silent, subtle struggles, however, can often be the most debilitating. Whether we're bound up in the grip of substance abuse or passing through life apathetic and despondent, we struggle to find ourselves. We all struggle to find that person we know we were created to be. And there is one thing I know we absolutely have in common and it is this, as the Bible states so well to help us envision the reality: "We all, like sheep, have gone astray, each of us has turned to his own way."[10]

You don't have to be a Derrik or an Andrew to experience radical change in your life. Some of the most dynamic Christian people are the ones who found Jesus at a young age. Or at a time when they thought that they were okay and life was humming along fine. But fine can be a misnomer. My own father, Luis Palau, began his relationship with God at the age of twelve. He wasn't a violent criminal or a stereotypical prodigal son, but he had a bad temper and a dirty mouth. He knew his position in life and in regard to eternity. When offered forgiveness, he took it knowing full well he'd been rescued.

Everyone, even my dad, needs to come to God the same way. Derrik and I shared a common backstory. That story made it clear that we needed to turn from the life path we were barreling down. And that's the first part of coming to Jesus: repentance—recognizing that I am wrong and that

God is right. Repentance is the rebel's only way to God. And we all are rebels.

At the heart of rebellion lies pride in its most cantankerous form. My rebellion grew haughtier the further I plunged into a depraved life. I was like the fourth-century North African theologian Augustine and his friends whose "pride was the more aggressive the more debauched their acts were." I reveled not only in the fulfillment of my lustful desires but also in the admiration my exploits garnered from my friends.

Augustine must have been a fine one to hang with in his heyday—drinking and fornicating his way into power among his peers. And that's what drove me toward the immoral: the power of pride.

I remember hearing stories of the garden of Eden as a young boy: how Eve took the fruit and ate it and then offered it to Adam. Adam and Eve wanted to be like God. Their pride and grab for power drove their rebellion. When they ate the fruit, the human race fell. Their pride and thirst for power plunged the created order into a tailspin, and we have been trying to overpower one another—and God—ever since.

### First Gospel

If we look a little closer at the garden of Eden story, however, we find more than rebellion. We find something else. Something cloaked in mystery, subtle and violent, yet beautiful in every way. If we're not careful, we can pass right over it.

After the act of rebellion by Adam and Eve, just before God expels them from the garden, God sets off a series of curses. And amid this sad listing of the results of their actions is an amazing phrase. God, speaking to Satan, says, "He will crush your head, and you will strike his heel."[11]

These are words of prophecy. When God tells Satan, "He will crush your head," the word *He* is referring to the promised, coming Messiah. A savior. The Messiah will defeat Satan with a crushing blow. But ironically, this death strike from the Messiah will not come from a political rebellion and revolution. It will not come with the advent of a new and glorious earthly kingdom the people could run to right then and there.

It will come on a cross.

The Messiah will become a curse to relieve the curse— "for cursed is anyone who hangs on a tree." And that's what a cross is—the execution tree for murderers and adulterers and thieves. Rebels. This is the Messiah's crushing blow. He uses Satan's lethal heel strike to overcome. Death to bring victory over death—sacrifice to pull us close, to restore our broken relationship with God.

This is our first glimpse of the gospel message in the whole Bible. God the Father is foretelling the death of His unique Son, Jesus, as the means to quell man's rebellion, allowing for the righting of relationships between God and humankind. The proper settling of the issue of sin and guilt—for rebels and for fools.

From this distant moment in the garden, God is telling you and me, "Rebellion cannot keep Me from pursuing you. And to prove it, I will not stop until sin is conquered. I will pursue you, though you run to the arms of the world, to the arms of selfishness, to the arms of other gods, I give the ultimate to offer the chance to once again walk and talk together."

What an astonishing thought.

More than a thought—it's the reality of the salvation God offers. In our contemporary society and in our self-reliance, we think we're the pursuers. We think we're the ones seeking God. But that's really just an excuse to light some candles and try to empty our minds of the chattering echoes. The end result—we stare at our navels in the dark.

God *alone* is the pursuer.

And He's already made a way for us to come to Him. But in the West, our affluence keeps us too busy ascending waiting lists for top-flight preschools and figuring out how to lease the bigger-SUV-with-better-gas-mileage to notice. I rarely noticed God's pursuit of me.

"Come to me, all you who are weary and burdened, and I will give you rest."[12]

It was right there the whole time. But I was too busy constructing my own personal rebellion; I walked right by Him. I had to go all the way to another country to finally get the point.

# TEN

# COMING TO GRIPS WITH LOVE

Christian love grants the beloved all his imperfections and weaknesses and in all his changes remains with him, loving the person it sees.

—Søren Kierkegaard

WHEN I SET out to change my life after I returned from Jamaica the first time, I went about it like a person trying to skip to the next chapter in a book. I wanted to stay on that story line and flip the page and move ahead instead of radically dealing with the old and picking up and starting again with the new. We hear people say it all the time: "Well, Andrew, you're starting a new chapter in life." But that analogy doesn't make sense to me now; that's not how it works. Sure, we move forward and away from our paths, but repentance represents picking up an entirely new book. The beautiful thing about all this "newness" language we're discussing here is: it's about starting fresh, but on God's terms. He begins to write a new story, washing the old and dirty you away.

But repentance does not focus only on the things we call vices or sinful living. Rather, it's recognizing who God is and who you are in light of that. It's the shocking revelation that God's magnificence envelops everything you've ever done. It is in the moment that we confess we are wrong and begin a new trajectory.

Often it's when we're fine that we find our lives unraveling beneath the surface. In the Western world, life can easily fool us with a veneer. We think the success we've found or our possessions pad our lives in such a way as to keep us from falling prey to the dark side of life.

But that's where we get snagged! The reality? This facade only keeps us from recognizing how deeply the darkness has seeped into our hearts. We live oblivious to where it lies beneath and how far from truth it's taken us. The Irish statesman Edmund Burke is credited with words to this effect: "The only thing necessary for evil to triumph is for good men to do nothing." What a sobering thought, especially when you read it in light of your own personal spiritual standing. By certain standards, you may be good or at least fine, but still need something more in order to keep the subtleties of evil at bay. By thinking we're okay, we end up cruising through life, doing nothing to deal with the things that cause us to struggle. Whether it's abuse or apathy or arrogance that haunts us, we all reach the point where we experience the void that's left when the world's promises, or lack thereof, leave us downtrodden. Something must be done. But no one else can reply to the call of God on our behalf. It's up to you. It's up to me.

The beauty about finding yourself in the ashes of life is the potential for new life. There's a passage in the Bible where God tells one of His followers, "Before I shaped you in the womb, I knew all about you. Before you saw the light of day, I had holy plans for you."[13] God's words here are true for us as well. And they encourage us in two ways.

First, when we find ourselves in those places where things in life are spiraling out of control and we feel alone, we know that God is thinking about us. In fact, we've been on God's mind since before we were born. In the book of Isaiah, God tells us,

"I've written your names on the backs of my hands."[14] That means that everything He puts His hand to, in all His responsibilities and cares—your face is constantly there before Him. It's natural for us to desire to be known and loved and accepted. God created us with those desires hardwired to our souls. God also fulfills them.

It's interesting to me that when things get dirty in life, we tend to cry out to God for help. I think we all know, somehow, deep down that God is always close by, that He always hears us when we call for help. We don't recognize our need for Him much when things are cruising along in life—when we're making the grade and getting the promotion, getting the girl or guy we want, or acquiring wealth and power. We think we don't need Him that much because we've actually stepped outside of our created purpose: to be in relationship with God. Replacing that relationship with worldly desires only leads to ruin. Recognizing we need Him in our lives to feel and know we're complete is the first step to understanding just how precious we are to Him.

Isaiah's verse also encourages us that our life has purpose, that God has a plan for our lives. When I came to terms with this fact, my life changed radically. I used to feel like I had to have it all together. I measured myself according to the world's standards for success. This mentality produced an unhealthy amount of anxiety, as I was constantly looking for that special place in this world, in this life. I carried the burden of trying to decide on my own what I was supposed to be and the person I would become.

I found peace when I stopped striving to fulfill some unspoken measurement of success that never settled in the same place two days in a row, and I began seeking God's plan for my life. His plan far exceeds anything I can produce on my own. When I truly began walking with God, my purpose in life was simplified. The biggest "Aha!" for me was discovering that God's plan and purpose for me does not revolve around compensation or location—what I do or where I live. It revolves around Him! The more intimate my relationship with God became, the more my goals and plans were shaped into His.

The first great realization in my journey of faith in Jesus Christ was coming to grips with God's love for me and His plan for my life.

## Taking God off the Shelf

As I began to feel at home in God's embrace—feeling found and known—I also began to understand how far I had actually strayed from the peace that God offers through Jesus. There's a spiritual death related to living outside of God's laws. I never noticed this growing up, but when you get to the edge of the ashen plains and see the green pastures on the other side, you can see the death around you for what it really is. I entered into all the relationships of the world, relationships with shame that *seemed* to say, "Now you are really living!" But when I realized I was choking on the ashes of it all, I saw death plain and haughty, staring me down.

The mother of a friend of mine used to comment to my mother how great we were. "Those boys are good boys," she'd say. "They're just sowing their wild oats. They are not bad kids like so-and-so." Lobbing the clichés.

My mom was proud of me. She could see that on the good works outweighing bad works, I might be able to lay a claim. But she loved me enough to face the fact that those are false scales. My mom could see death for what it was.

"Can't you see that they *look* like good boys because they're experts at hiding who they really are? They aren't *living* like good boys. Sowing your wild oats isn't justification for reckless living."

Mom had X-ray vision. The idea that we weren't hurting anyone was nonsense to her. We were hurting our mothers—

oh, the weight of knowing that. We hurt our fathers too—that was bad enough. Recklessness produces wreckage—like the wreckage I crawled out of on the Jamaican runway—wrecked lives and collateral damage. Reckless living could mean physical death, depending on the situation, but it certainly means spiritual death in every situation. For years that didn't matter so much to me because I felt I was invincible; all the wreckage could be hidden. Haven't we all felt we could hide it?

Growing up I heard my dad talk about the things that "lead to death." We think of things that don't visibly hurt anyone, such as pornography and casual sex, and forget that disease and abortion and depression can sit on the other side of the fence. These things actually lead to death, and that death weighs on so many of us; these things are the fruit that is borne out of the wreckage that we choose to cultivate in our lives.

All this that we hide, I honestly don't care what you might call it; I often call it the garbage of my life. God calls it sin. It seeps into the soil and lingers in the root of our being. We cannot escape our natural proclivity for sin. Theologians and great writers make their living plumbing the depths of the concept. Kierkegaard said that sin is anything that we put up in place of God. Like a wall of shelves lined with trinkets and goodies that we love, and then right there, on the bottom, the God-trinket sits. God is no trinket. Yet we have constructed a nice little box-trinket that we've labeled "God." We think we can somehow stuff Him in there.

We set it next to all the other trinkets. It collects dust like all the other trinkets. We forget about it sitting down there. We've put everything else in life above it—above God.

That is the definition of sin: making gods out of our own selves or the things for which we desperately long.

When I could finally identify what sin was in my life and how it gripped me, I was able to see its grip released and was able to turn toward something else. I heard my father talk about this concept too. He called it *confession*. As children our parents ask us, "Did you break that window with the baseball?" When we admit guilt—which is hard to do when you're a cool kid with an ego the size of a VW Bug—we confess. Consequences ensue, but so does forgiveness. This is what I experienced with God when I finally said, "Yes, I was wrong in all of that stuff." When I finally stopped harboring my sin and wreckage, I could breathe again. I was healed of many addictions on the spot, and others have progressively been addressed and continue to fade. My relationships began to mend, and I was finally able to embrace my true identity: child of God.

## Confronting Our Shadows

I recently met with a group of men and we discussed life and family and struggles and victories. During our conversation I could sense that Sam felt unnerved or uncomfortable. We had discussed pornography for a few moments and moved on to other topics. But it seemed Sam was disappointed we had moved on so quickly. I sensed that he recognized an opportunity to come clean on something that was weighing him down. I didn't say anything, and the conversation progressed and we left.

As I drove home, I wondered about Sam. I wondered about our discussion. *Why don't we talk about the things that really haunt us in life?* I think we fail in our trust for one another. And that failure forces our hands, so we keep darkness in our lives behind closed doors. Where is the freedom for us to open the door and cast light into our shadowy corners? It doesn't exist. Because we lock up our spirits.

For me, locking myself up meant focusing on no one else. My ambition and my desires took center stage. I fit in well with what the world deemed to be acceptable, even successful. Many of us end up there, alone in the black of night, promoting our pride to salve the pain of previous action and experience.

The brother of Jesus said that wherever we find selfish ambition, "there you find disorder and every evil practice."[15] In order to reach the place where I could confess anything to God, I had to deal with selfish ambition and envy. I could not fathom the thought of crawling out of the pit I had dug for myself. I didn't deserve it. If God was real, why would He even want me? Was I not an embarrassment to my family and to myself? Then I stumbled across this little section in the Bible. The apostle Paul wrote it. I think he knew a thing or two about newness.

> Because of this decision we don't evaluate people by what they have or how they look. We looked at the Messiah that way once and got it all wrong, as you know. We certainly don't look at him that way anymore. Now we look inside, and what we see is that anyone united with the Messiah gets a fresh start, is created new. The old life is gone; a new life burgeons! Look at it!
>
> How? you ask. In Christ. God put the wrong on Him who never did anything wrong, so we could be put right with God.[16]

He's talking to you and this offer remains for you. He's ready to befriend you. Will you befriend Him? Imagine this reality being yours. Your sins are forgiven. Your burdens are shared. The old has gone, your sin is remembered no more. Your powerlessness, your fear? It's gone. It is no more.

Is this not a radical thought?

How could I, a man who had thrown off what I knew to be right for lies and deceit, be new? How could I as a man who had done such awful things with women—taken advantage of their kindness and willingness to be with me—be new? How could I, a man who had earned the moniker "Ten Drugs," who climbed down into the depths of self-induced stupors, be new? How is it possible to reach into me as a person and pull out goodness? Where is it? How does it exist?

The more I think of it, the more I write out the words of my life, the more dumbfounded I become. My situation does not deserve a helping hand from God. If a future waits for me, it should be a future of loss and loneliness. Right?

Those thoughts are devilishness seeping into the brain. To keep us at bay from God, to keep us from encountering the love He freely offers, the devil whispers his sweet nothings—and that's what they are. Nothings! For if I believe them, I too will become and stay as one who is nothing.

There is a film about the life and conversion of Martin Luther—the sixteenth-century monk known for starting Protestantism. Early in the film, Luther stands at a spiritual crossroads. He sees what the church deemed to be "religion," but he knew that this was not, could not, be God.

In one scene, his spiritual father overhears him violently praying to God in one of the prayer rooms, desperately trying to rid himself of all his sin. Why? Luther lives in fear of God because he believes Him to be nothing more than "a righteous judge who damns us." His mentor enters the prayer room and confronts him by asking Luther what he wants from God. "A God whom I can love," Luther replies. "A God who loves me."

The older monk comforts Luther and tells him, "You think that self-hatred will save you . . . but you're just not honest. God is not angry with you. You are angry with God." Luther then pleads for guidance from his mentor.

"Bind yourself to Christ; say to Him, 'I am Yours. Save me.'"

*I am Yours. Save me.*

Those words climb into my heart as I think of how desperately I was in need of saving yet with little power to admit it. Like Luther, I tried using everything else to save me, while all along I simply needed to ask. Near the end of the film

Luther must present himself before the highest officials and recant his writings on the grace of God. Uncharacteristically, Luther is unable to speak his heart to the high council and asks for one night to consider his response.

The scene is reminiscent of the earlier one—the monk prays late into the night, wrestling with the devil and with God. At the end of this intense scene, the camera pulls back, showing the monk face-down in the prayer room repeating: "I am Yours. Save me. I am Yours. Save me. I am Yours . . . save me."

Grab me, Jesus, from the lies whispered to me now. I am no longer that man in the bars, passed out in the alleyway, lost in Europe, and lost from You. I am no longer that foolhardy dervish. I am no longer that frightened man, scared to be alone with my thoughts. Thank You! I am Yours!

I am Yours.

# YOUR INVITATION FROM GOD

COME TO ME, ALL YOU WHO ARE WEARY AND
BURDENED, AND I WILL GIVE YOU REST.
MATTHEW 11:28


WE'RE ALL LIKE SHEEP WHO'VE WANDERED OFF
AND GOTTEN LOST. WE'VE ALL DONE OUR OWN
THING, GONE OUR OWN WAY. AND GOD HAS PILED
ALL
OUR SINS, EVERYTHING WE'VE DONE WRONG,
ON HIM, ON HIM.
ISAIAH 53:6 MSG


IF WE CONFESS OUR SINS, HE IS FAITHFUL AND
JUST TO FORGIVE US OUR SINS AND TO CLEANSE
US FROM ALL UNRIGHTEOUSNESS.
1 JOHN 1:9 ESV


IF YOU DECLARE WITH YOUR MOUTH, "JESUS IS
LORD," AND BELIEVE IN YOUR HEART THAT GOD
RAISED HIM FROM THE DEAD, YOU WILL BE SAVED.
ROMANS 10:9


TO ALL WHO DID RECEIVE HIM, TO THOSE WHO
BELIEVED IN HIS NAME, HE GAVE THE RIGHT
TO BECOME CHILDREN OF GOD.
JOHN 1:12

# ACKNOWLEDGMENTS

**Thanks//**
**Heavenly Father** – for loving me and never giving up on me.

**Wendy** – my wife, friend, and partner in life, for life. You are a brilliant reflection of God to me and to so many.

**Chris, Jonathan, and Sadie** – my beautiful children. You fill my life with fun and meaning. Walk with God.

**Dad and Mom** – You took the message to the world and never forgot *the one*. This story is more about you and your faithfulness than it is about me.

To all my friends who shared this story with me:
**LPA Board of Directors, Team members, and all the Palau, Levy, and McKeehan families** – It is a privilege to have friends and family who work and serve together in the furthering of the Good News. Now that's living life to the fullest.

**Tim and Chris Willard** – More than just hard work, writing skills, and techniques, you poured your very selves into this book, believing in it and making it possible.

**Matt Yates** – Many warm thanks for the confidence and capacity you drew out and instilled across the board.

**Worthy Publishing** – for your faith in this project. From the very start to the last edit, your team has supported and encouraged with great patience. This book was strengthened greatly by your thoughtfulness and insights.

# NOTES

[1] "Jesus, Name above All Names," by Naida Hearn. © 1974, 1978 Scriptures in Song (admin. by Maranatha! Music). All rights reserved.

[2] John 16:32-33 ESV.

[3] *Alive*, directed by Frank Marshall (Burbank, CA: Touchstone Pictures, 1993).

[4] Hebrews 6:1.

[5] Ralph Waldo Emerson, "Self-Reliance," *Essays and English Traits*: vol. 5 (New York: P. F. Collier and Son Company, 1909-14).

[6] "Empire State of Mind" by Shawn Carter, Angela Hunte, Jane't Sewell-Ulepic, et. al. © 2009 Roc Nation/Atlantic. All rights reserved.

[7] Francis Thompson, "The Hound of Heaven," http://www.bartleby.com/236/239.html

[8] Romans 12:1-3.

[9] Isaiah 6:1-8 MSG.

[10] Isaiah 53:6.

[11] Genesis 3:15.

[12] Matthew 11:28.

[13] Jeremiah 1:5 MSG.

[14] Isaiah 49:16 MSG.

[15] James 3:16.

[16] 2 Corinthians 5:16-21 MSG.

IF THIS BOOK HAS ENCOURAGED OR
IMPACTED YOU OR SOMEONE YOU KNOW,
I WOULD LOVE TO HEAR FROM YOU.
YOU CAN CONTACT ME AT:

THE PALAU ASSOCIATION
PO Box 50
Portland, OR 97207
USA

YOU MAY ALSO CONNECT WITH ME VIA:
WEB: www.palau.org
EMAIL: info@palau.org
PHONE: 503.614.1500

FACEBOOK: www.facebook.com/andrewpalau

## ANDREW PALAU,

son of international evangelist Luis Palau, is an evangelist in his own right—organizing global outreach events for the Palau Association and regularly sharing the gospel with tens of thousands of people. Andrew can be heard on the daily radio program *Reaching Your World*, which is on more than 850 radio stations in 27 countries. He and the Palau team have also been featured in some of the world's leading media outlets including the Associated Press, *Forbes Online*, the *Washington Post*, CNBC Asia, and *USA Today*. In addition, Andrew maintains his own website, which receives 5,000 visitors a month. He and his wife, Wendy, have three children and live in Portland, Oregon, close to the world headquarters of the Palau ministry.

WORTHY
PUBLISHING

## IF YOU LIKED THIS BOOK . . .

- Tell your friends by going to: www.thesecretlife ofafool.com and clicking "LIKE"

- Share the video book trailer by posting it on your Facebook page

- Head over to our Facebook page, click "LIKE" and post a comment regarding what you enjoyed about the book

- Tweet "I recommend reading #SecretLifeOfAFool by @andrewpalau @Worthypub"

- Hashtag: #SecretLifeOfAFool

- Subscribe to our newsletter by going to http://worthypublishing.com/about/subscribe.php

WORTHY PUBLISHING
FACEBOOK PAGE

WORTHY PUBLISHING
WEBSITE

Hard to imagine the severity of the storm and the raging of the sea as the tranquil beauty of Jamaica broke back through the very next morning after the crash. A lot like how life can be, yes?

Drove by the next day and was able to take this shot out of my father-in-law's sunroof. Notice the location of the right-side engine in both pictures.

*Ouch!* Twenty-seven stitches between the eyes.

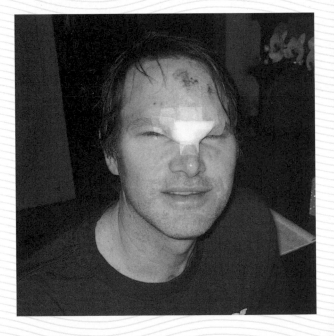

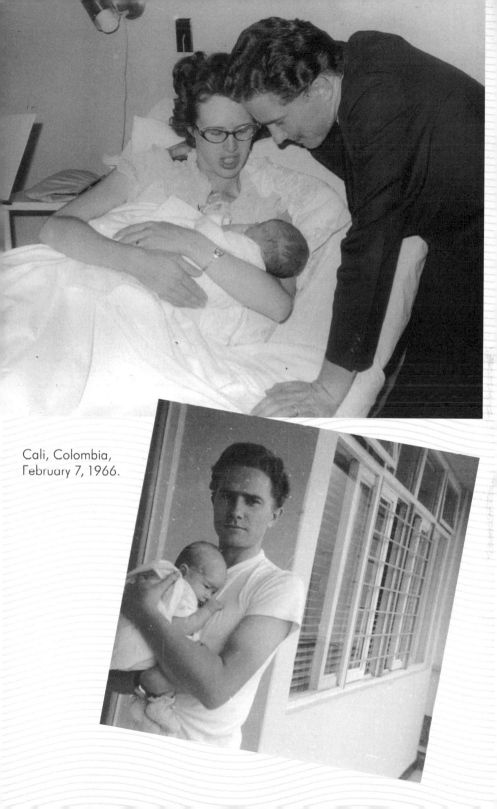

Cali, Colombia,
February 7, 1966.

Dad, Mom, my brothers, and I still connect to this day with a deep joy evident in these photos.

Luis Palau's first outreach…
festival… call it what you will.
Bogota, Colombia, 1966.

While Dad was
preaching around
the world, Mom
held down the fort!

¡FELIZ NAVIDAD!

1973

Luis and Pat
Kevin, Andrew, Stephen. Keith

Missionary Christmas card: Good intentions, Bible in hand, but a dirty mouth.

Easter in Grandpa and Grandma Scofield's back yard. Above those West Hills of Portland, God revealed an image of heaven to me—the first call to come and follow Him.

How did we get from here...

...to here?

Nothing wrong with fishing! Love it to this day, but my early priorities were all wrong.

No room for extra weight while hitchhiking through Europe. An aluminum Johnny Walker cap served as a glass in France.

Diving off the rocks with *clochard* village just around the corner. The warmth of the days fooled us into thinking we'd be warm at night on the beach...

... but the crack of dawn drove us out from under the sailboat to seek wind-free spots of warmth where we could find them.

A constant lifeline, these letters from my dad are a treasure.

Here's Chris fighting the very marlin that lured me out to Jamaica. It took us by surprise—no fighting belt, let alone a fighting chair.

Dad, the quintessential "fisher of men." In the midst of that crowd at Kingston National Stadium, it was just God and me.

It didn't take a genius to see that there was some interest between these two.

On the veranda of the cottage, amongst coffee fields in the Blue Mountains. Amazingly, someone took a photo only moments after my encounter with God. A lot to take in, hence the stunned look. That moment of decision has led to a lifetime of growth, adjustments, and very, very great blessing.

And the greatest of them all, my sweet Wendy.

...and my three children.

Now, I'll never stop fishing.